THE QUANTUM GUARD

Redefining Security and Privacy in the Age

of AI and Quantum Computing

Written By.

TROY WILLIAMS

CONTENTS

INTRODUCTION

MY JOURNEY: FROM CYBERSECURITY TO QUANTUM COMPUTING

Every journey begins with a single step, and mine started in a rather unexpected place: RadioShack. In the early 1990s, I managed a store in Lebanon, Tennessee, selling electronics and helping customers solve everyday problems. But even then, something more significant was brewing beneath the surface of this retail environment. Customers frequently asked about recording devices, and it quickly became apparent that many of them were attempting to catch a cheating spouse. These interactions, while ordinary at the time, ignited my curiosity about privacy, security, and the digital footprint we leave behind. It wasn't just about gadgets; it was about the information they could collect and how it could be used.

This curiosity led me to take a leap of faith, a jump that would change the trajectory of my career and life. On a coin toss, I decided to leave retail and pursue a career as a private investigator (PI). That decision marked the beginning of my immersion into the world of investigations, where I dealt with everything from domestic cases to criminal investigations. As a PI, I quickly learned that information was power, and those who controlled access to information could wield enormous influence, for good or ill. I became deeply interested in how data, susceptible personal data, could be exploited or protected.

In the early days, investigations were a blend of legwork and intuition. But as the internet began to evolve, so did the tools and techniques at my disposal. I witnessed firsthand the shift from paper trails to digital footprints, from physical evidence to metadata, and from one-on-one interviews to analyzing emails and digital records. The internet was becoming a double-edged sword, a tool for solving cases, and a growing source of risk for individuals and businesses.

As the world moved further into the digital age, I saw an opportunity to leverage my investigative skills in a new and rapidly growing field: cybersecurity. It wasn't enough to gather evidence; now, it was about preventing the breaches, attacks, and data thefts that were becoming alarmingly common. By the mid-2000s, I had transitioned fully into cybersecurity, and it felt like a natural progression. Cybersecurity, in many ways, was the new frontier of private investigations. The criminals were no longer just in dark alleys; they were hiding behind screens, launching attacks from across the world, and exploiting weaknesses in systems we had come to trust.

This shift wasn't without its challenges. The early days of cybersecurity were reactive by nature. We focused on securing perimeters, using firewalls and antivirus software to protect systems from known threats. Every time a new attack emerged, whether it was a virus, malware, or phishing scheme, we worked tirelessly to close the gap. It was a game of cat and mouse, always trying to stay one step ahead of the attackers. But over time, it became clear that this reactive approach wasn't enough. The threats were evolving faster than our defenses, and we needed a new way to think about security.

My interest in more proactive approaches to security led me to the Zero Trust model, a transformative framework that assumes no one inside or outside the network can be trusted. This concept resonated deeply with me, as it aligned with my experience as a PI. Trust, after all, was something that had to be earned, not given unquestioningly. In the digital realm, Trust has become a liability. Zero Trust meant verifying every connection, every access request, and every piece of data flowing through a system. It was about shifting from defense to offense, anticipating threats, and neutralizing them before they could cause harm.

It was around this time that I began to delve deeper into AI and its applications in cybersecurity. Artificial intelligence presented a new way to think about the challenges we face. Instead of reacting to threats, AI allows us to predict them. Machine learning algorithms could analyze vast amounts of data in real time, identifying patterns and anomalies that would be impossible for human operators to detect. This was a game-changer. The idea of having an AI system that could learn, adapt, and protect against threats in real time was not just appealing; it was essential. The world of cybersecurity was becoming too complex for traditional methods alone, and AI was the tool that could help us regain the upper hand.

But the more I explored AI, the more I realized that the actual future of security lies in a technology still in its infancy: quantum computing. While AI could help us manage today's challenges, quantum computing has the potential to revolutionize the entire landscape. Quantum computing is fundamentally different from classical computing. It operates on principles of quantum mechanics, using qubits that can represent multiple states simultaneously. This allows quantum computers to solve problems that would take classical computers thousands or even millions of years to crack.

As I dug into quantum computing, I quickly understood its dual-edged nature. On the one hand, it promised to break traditional encryption methods, raising concerns about the security of all data currently protected by encryption. On the other hand, it offered the possibility of creating unbreakable encryption methods using quantum mechanics. This was the future of cybersecurity; quantum encryption could protect data in ways we could only dream of with classical systems.

The transition from traditional cybersecurity to quantum-driven solutions felt inevitable. Quantum computing is not just an advancement in processing power; it represents a complete overhaul of how we approach data protection, encryption, and even AI itself. Quantum computers will be able to run AI algorithms that are orders of magnitude more potent than what we use today, unlocking new potential for predictive security systems, biometrics, and real-time threat detection.

Throughout my journey, one thing has remained constant: the need to stay ahead of the curve. From the days of investigating cheating spouses with essential recording devices to tackling complex cybersecurity threats, I've always believed in looking forward to the next technology, the next threat, and the next solution. Today, that means embracing AI and quantum computing as the keys to redefining how we protect our most valuable resource: data.

In this book, I want to share not only my journey but also the lessons I've learned along the way. The world of cybersecurity is constantly evolving, and those of us in the field must evolve with it. As we move into the age of AI and quantum computing, the challenges will only grow more complex, but so will the opportunities to build a safer, more secure digital world. The future of security and privacy is unfolding before our eyes, and this book will help you understand and prepare for the revolution that's already underway.

FRAMING THE QUANTUM FUTURE: SECURITY, PRIVACY, AND AI

We are standing at a pivotal moment in history when the rise of quantum computing and artificial intelligence (AI) transformed how we think about security and privacy. These technologies, which were once the subject of science fiction, are now fundamental tools reshaping the digital landscape. But with this transformation comes both opportunities and challenges. To understand the future of security and privacy, we must first grasp how AI and quantum computing will change the way we protect our data, secure our systems, and manage the flow of information in the digital age.

The Role of AI in Modern Security

Artificial intelligence has already started revolutionizing cybersecurity. In the past, security systems relied heavily on human oversight and manual processes. Security experts had to monitor systems for potential threats, often reacting after a breach had already occurred. This reactive approach was slow and left many systems vulnerable to attacks that were becoming more sophisticated every day.

AI has flipped that model on its head by introducing proactive security measures. Through machine learning and data analysis, AI systems can now predict, identify, and neutralize threats before they cause damage. These systems can monitor vast amounts of data in real time, learning from patterns of behavior and detecting unusual activities that might signal an attack. AI doesn't sleep, doesn't take breaks, and can process more information in a single moment than any human could in a lifetime. This makes AI a powerful tool in the fight against cyber threats.

For example, AI can analyze data traffic across a network and flag any suspicious behavior. If someone tries to access a system from an unusual location or performs actions outside of their routine, AI can alert security teams or automatically block access. This real-time analysis means that companies and individuals can protect their sensitive information before a hacker has the chance to exploit a vulnerability.

However, while AI provides incredible security benefits, it also raises new concerns about privacy. AI systems require access to large amounts of data to learn and improve, which means that personal information is often part of the equation. This creates a delicate balance between using AI to protect data and ensuring that the data itself isn't being misused or exposed to risks.

Quantum Computing: The Next Frontier in Data Security

Quantum computing is set to be the next revolutionary force in the tech world. Unlike classical computers, which use bits to process information as 0s and 1s, quantum computers use qubits. These qubits can exist in multiple states simultaneously, allowing quantum computers to process data at speeds that are unimaginable with today's technology. For example, a problem that would take a classical computer thousands of years to solve could be completed by a quantum computer in minutes.

While this is exciting for advancements in science, medicine, and engineering, it poses a significant challenge for cybersecurity. Much of the encryption we rely on today, whether to secure bank accounts, personal emails, or government secrets, is based on the limitations of classical computing. It would take a regular computer far too long to break these encryption methods. But a quantum computer could crack many of these codes quickly, potentially exposing vast amounts of sensitive data.

This is why the development of quantum-safe encryption is critical. Researchers are already working on creating encryption methods that are resistant to quantum attacks, ensuring that our future digital systems remain secure even as quantum computing becomes more common. Quantum encryption uses the principles of quantum mechanics to create codes that are nearly impossible to break. One example is quantum key distribution (QKD), a technique that uses the behavior of quantum particles to transmit encryption keys securely. Any attempt to intercept these keys would alter their state, immediately signaling a breach.

While quantum computing challenges current security models, it also provides new opportunities. The same power that makes quantum computing a threat to traditional encryption also makes it a tool for developing more robust, more secure systems. Quantum encryption could revolutionize how we protect data, ensuring that it stays safe even in the face of future technological advances.

Privacy in the Age of AI and Quantum Computing

As AI and quantum computing reshape security, they also raise critical questions about privacy. In today's world, data is constantly being collected, whether it's through our smartphones, social media accounts, or even smart home devices. AI systems require access to vast amounts of data to function effectively. This data is used to train AI models, improve accuracy, and make predictions. But as these systems become more powerful, how do we ensure that personal data remains protected?

One of the biggest concerns is the potential misuse of data. Companies and governments may use AI to collect and analyze personal information without individuals fully understanding how their data is being used. This has already led to scandals involving the misuse of data for political campaigns or targeted advertising. As AI becomes more integrated into our daily lives, it is crucial to establish clear guidelines for data collection and use to prevent abuses of privacy.

Quantum computing adds another layer to this issue. While it offers the potential for unbreakable encryption, it also raises the stakes for data security. If quantum computers can break existing encryption, any data that has been collected and stored could suddenly become vulnerable. This makes it more critical than ever to think about privacy from the ground up, ensuring that the systems we build today are designed to protect personal information long into the future.

Balancing Innovation with Responsibility

The future of security and privacy will depend on our ability to balance innovation with responsibility. AI and quantum computing offer incredible tools for protecting data, but they also create new risks that must be carefully managed. As we develop these technologies, we must ensure that they are used to enhance security without compromising privacy.

To do this, we need to create a framework that prioritizes privacy from the beginning. This means developing AI systems that are transparent about how data is used, creating encryption methods that are resilient to quantum attacks, and establishing ethical guidelines for the use of these technologies. Governments, companies, and individuals all have a role to play in shaping the future of privacy and security.

Ultimately, the goal is to create a future where technology works for us. AI and quantum computing protect our data, secure our systems, and ensure our privacy without sacrificing our freedoms. If we can achieve this balance, we will not only harness the power of these technologies but also build a safer, more secure digital world.

PART 1: FOUNDATIONS OF ARTIFICIAL INTELLIGENCE AND QUANTUM COMPUTING

UNDERSTANDING ARTIFICIAL INTELLIGENCE (AI)

Artificial Intelligence (AI) refers to the simulation of human intelligence in machines that are designed to think, learn, and make decisions, much like humans do. It's a broad field of computer science that involves creating systems capable of performing tasks that typically require human cognitive abilities, such as problem-solving, recognizing patterns, understanding language, and making decisions. What sets AI apart from traditional computing is its ability to learn from experiences and adapt over time, which gives it the potential to solve problems that are far too complex for simple rule-based systems.

At its core, AI systems are built to analyze data, detect patterns, and make predictions or decisions based on the information they process. Instead of being programmed with specific instructions for every possible situation, AI systems are trained to "learn" by analyzing vast amounts of data. Through this learning process, AI can improve its performance over time, becoming more accurate and efficient as it processes more data.

Types of Artificial Intelligence

AI is generally divided into two broad categories:

1. **Narrow AI (Weak AI):** This is the form of AI that we see most commonly in the world today. Narrow AI is designed to perform a single or limited range of tasks. It can process specific functions like image recognition, language translation, or driving a car, but it cannot perform functions outside of its designated purpose. For example,

your smartphone's virtual assistant, such as Siri or Google Assistant, is a form of narrow AI. These assistants can perform a range of tasks, such as setting reminders or answering questions, but they do not have the broad, general intelligence to perform unrelated tasks.

2. **General AI (Strong AI):** General AI, which is still theoretical, refers to machines that possess the ability to perform any intellectual task that a human can do. Unlike narrow AI, which is limited to a specific function, General AI would be able to learn, reason, and adapt to a wide variety of tasks across different domains. It would not be confined to one specific area of expertise. This type of AI remains mainly in the realm of science fiction today, but it represents the goal of many researchers in the AI field.

DIGITAL SECURITY SHIELD

Historical Milestones in AI Development

Artificial Intelligence (AI) has come a long way since its inception. What began as theoretical ideas about machines mimicking human intelligence have grown into a transformative force that impacts nearly every sector of society. Notable breakthroughs, setbacks, and paradigm shifts mark the journey of AI development.

The concept of artificial intelligence was first formally introduced in the mid-20th century. In 1950, Alan Turing, a British mathematician, proposed the idea that machines could "think" in his landmark paper, "Computing Machinery and Intelligence." In this paper, Turing introduced what is now known as the Turing Test, a way to measure a machine's ability to exhibit intelligent behavior equivalent to, or indistinguishable from, that of a human. This concept laid the foundation for the field of AI by raising philosophical and practical questions about the nature of intelligence.

In 1956, the term "artificial intelligence" was officially coined during the Dartmouth Conference, organized by computer scientist John McCarthy. McCarthy, along with other pioneers like Marvin Minsky, Claude Shannon, and Herbert Simon, gathered to discuss the possibility of creating machines capable of simulating every aspect of human learning and intelligence. This conference is widely considered the birth of AI as an academic discipline.

Early AI research during this period focused on symbolic AI, also known as good old-fashioned AI (GOFAI), where machines were programmed to solve problems using symbolic reasoning. These systems were rule-based and relied heavily on formal logic. One notable achievement during this time was the development of the Logic Theorist, a program created by Allen Newell and Herbert A. Simon in 1956. The Logic Theorist could prove mathematical theorems, marking one of the first instances where a machine exhibited reasoning capabilities like human logic.

The initial enthusiasm surrounding AI in the 1960s began to fade as researchers realized the limitations of early AI systems. While these systems could perform specific tasks, they struggled to scale or adapt to more complex problems. As a result, the 1970s and 1980s were marked by a period of disillusionment known as the "AI Winter."

During the AI Winter, progress slowed as funding dried up and interest waned. Early AI systems were too rigid and incapable of learning from new data. During this period, they have exposed the shortcomings of rule-based systems and the inability of AI to handle real-world uncertainties. Additionally, the limitations of computing power and the complexity of human intelligence posed significant obstacles to further advancements in the field.

Despite this setback, some progress was made in specialized AI applications. One of the notable achievements during this time was the development of expert systems. These systems were designed to emulate the decision-making abilities of human experts in specific fields, such as medicine or engineering. An example of an early expert system was MYCIN, which was developed in the 1970s to assist doctors in diagnosing bacterial infections and recommending treatments. Expert systems proved that AI could be useful in narrowly defined areas, but they lacked the flexibility and adaptability of general intelligence.

The AI Winter began to thaw in the 1980s with the resurgence of interest in machine learning and the development of artificial neural networks. While symbolic AI had focused on explicitly programmed rules, machine learning offered a new approach: systems that could learn from data rather than rely on pre-programmed rules. Advances inspired this shift in statistics, data processing, and computing power.

Artificial neural networks were modeled after the human brain, with layers of artificial neurons (also known as nodes) that could be trained to recognize patterns in data. These networks were capable of "learning" by adjusting the strength of connections between neurons based on input data. Early successes in neural networks included backpropagation, an algorithm that allowed networks to adapt their parameters to minimize errors automatically.

The 1990s saw a significant AI breakthrough when IBM's Deep Blue defeated world chess champion Garry Kasparov in 1997. This landmark event demonstrated AI's potential to master complex strategic games. While Deep Blue's victory was based on brute-force computation and not machine learning, it was a clear sign that AI was making progress in tackling high-level cognitive tasks.

At the same time, AI research began to expand into areas like natural language processing (NLP), computer vision, and robotics. These advancements laid the groundwork for the AI boom that was to come in the 21st century.

The 2000s marked the beginning of AI's rapid expansion, mainly driven by advances in machine learning and big data. Machine learning algorithms, which allow systems to learn patterns from large datasets, have become the dominant approach to AI development. As data collection became more ubiquitous (thanks to the internet, smartphones, and social media), AI systems could now be trained on vast amounts of real-world data.

One of the most significant developments during this period was deep learning, a subset of machine learning that utilizes multi-layered neural networks to analyze data. Deep learning allowed AI systems to achieve remarkable accuracy in tasks like image recognition, speech recognition, and natural language processing. For example, Google's DeepMind developed AlphaGo, a program that defeated the world champion of the game Goa feat, which is considered much more complex than chess due to the vast number of possible moves. AlphaGo's success in 2016 marked a new milestone in AI's ability to solve highly complex problems.

Speech recognition and natural language processing also made significant strides, with AI systems like Siri, Alexa, and Google Assistant becoming household names. Thanks to AI-driven advancements in understanding human language, these virtual assistants can understand voice commands, answer questions, and perform tasks.

Another significant leap forward came in the field of self-driving cars, with companies like Tesla, Waymo, and Uber developing autonomous vehicles powered by AI. These systems use a combination of sensors, cameras, and machine learning algorithms to navigate roads, detect obstacles, and make real-time decisions, pushing AI closer to real-world applications.

Today, AI is not just a tool but a crucial element in fields such as healthcare, finance, cybersecurity, and more. In healthcare, AI systems can analyze medical images, predict disease outbreaks, and even suggest personalized treatment plans. In finance, AI is used for fraud detection, algorithmic trading, and risk management. AI's application in cybersecurity helps identify potential threats, analyze malware, and predict future attacks, making it a key player in the defense against digital crime.

Today, AI is everywhere. From self-driving cars to predictive algorithms used by companies like Amazon and Google, AI touches nearly every aspect of modern life. The key to AI's success lies in machine learning, a subset of AI that allows machines to learn from data without being explicitly programmed.

In machine learning, AI systems are trained on vast amounts of data. They use this data to identify patterns and make decisions. For instance, when you watch a movie on Netflix, the system learns from your viewing habits and suggests similar content based on patterns it has detected in the behavior of other users.

Looking ahead, researchers are exploring Artificial General Intelligence (AGI)systems that can understand, learn, and apply intelligence across a broad range of tasks, much like humans can. While AGI remains a distant goal, the progress being made in narrow AI continues to accelerate.

AI's potential for growth is limitless, but it also presents ethical challenges. The rise of AI-driven surveillance, concerns about data privacy, and the displacement of jobs due to automation are all issues that society must address as AI continues to evolve.

How AI Works: Learning from Data

AI systems learn through a process known as machine learning, a subset of AI that allows systems to improve their performance over time without being explicitly programmed. Machine learning enables machines to analyze data, detect patterns, and make decisions based on that data.

To understand how AI systems learn, it's essential to look at the concept of training data. AI models are fed large datasets, which allow them to recognize patterns and make predictions. For example, if an AI system is being trained to identify cats in pictures, it will be fed thousands of images labeled as either "cat" or "not cat." By analyzing these images, the AI system learns to distinguish between features that define them, such as the shape of ears, eyes, and whiskers, and features that belong to other objects. Over time, the AI system becomes better at identifying cats in new, unseen images.

This process is not restricted to image recognition. AI can be trained on any type of data, including text, speech, video, and structured data like numbers. The key lies in the model's ability to learn from its mistakes and adjust its internal parameters to improve its accuracy over time.

Core Components of AI

Several core technologies power AI systems, allowing them to perform tasks that were once thought impossible for machines. These technologies include:

- Machine Learning (ML): Machine learning is the backbone of AI. It is the process through which AI systems learn from data, identify patterns, and make decisions. Unlike traditional programming, where specific instructions are given for every task, machine learning allows

AI systems to "figure things out" based on the data they receive. There are various types of machine learning, including supervised learning (where the system is trained on labeled data), unsupervised learning (where the system identifies patterns in unlabeled data), and reinforcement learning (where the system learns by receiving rewards or penalties based on its actions).

- Natural Language Processing (NLP): NLP is the technology that allows machines to understand and interact with human language. This includes tasks such as language translation, speech recognition, and text analysis. Systems like chatbots and virtual assistants rely heavily on NLP to interpret and respond to user input in natural language. The goal of NLP is to enable AI to understand the nuances of human language, including grammar, context, and sentiment.

- Neural Networks: Neural networks are a crucial component of deep learning, a subset of machine learning. Modeled after the human brain, neural networks consist of layers of nodes (neurons) that process and transform data. Each layer performs a specific function, passing its output to the next layer until the final output is generated. This architecture allows neural networks to solve complex problems, such as image recognition and speech processing. Neural networks are highly effective for tasks that involve pattern recognition and large amounts of unstructured data.

- Computer Vision: Computer vision is the field of AI that focuses on enabling machines to interpret and understand visual information from the world. It involves automatic extraction, analysis, and understanding of useful information from images and videos.

Applications of computer vision include facial recognition, object detection, and medical image analysis.

- Robotics: AI is also used in robotics to create machines that can perform physical tasks autonomously or semi-autonomously. AI-powered robots can be found in manufacturing, healthcare, logistics, and even homes. These robots use AI to navigate environments, recognize objects, and perform complex tasks such as assembling products or assisting in surgeries.

AI in Everyday Life

AI has made its way into many aspects of our daily lives, often in ways that we may not even notice. Some typical applications of AI include:

- Virtual Assistants: AI-powered virtual assistants like Siri, Google Assistant, and Alexa use natural language processing to understand and respond to spoken commands. They can set reminders, send texts, control smart home devices, and even provide answers to complex questions.

- Recommendation Systems: Platforms like Netflix, Amazon, and YouTube use AI algorithms to analyze user behavior and recommend content based on individual preferences. These recommendation systems are an example of how AI uses data to predict what users are likely to enjoy based on past interactions.

- Healthcare Diagnostics: AI is revolutionizing healthcare by helping doctors diagnose diseases more accurately and efficiently. AI algorithms can analyze medical images, detect abnormalities, and even predict the likelihood of diseases like cancer based on patient data. This improves early detection and allows for more personalized treatments.

- Self-Driving Cars: Autonomous vehicles rely on AI to navigate roads, interpret traffic signals, and avoid obstacles. Self-driving cars use a combination of computer vision, neural networks, and machine learning to operate safely without human intervention.

Machine Learning and Deep Learning Explained

What is Machine Learning?

Machine learning is a subset of artificial intelligence (AI) that enables computers to learn and make decisions without being explicitly programmed. Instead of following predefined rules, machine learning algorithms identify patterns in data, analyze them, and make predictions or decisions based on that analysis. It's about teaching machines to learn from experience, like how humans learn from trial and error.

The key to machine learning lies in data. The more data a machine learning model has access to, the more accurate and refined its predictions become. This is why companies like Google, Amazon, and Netflix collect vast amounts of data to improve the performance of their machine-learning models, making their services more innovative and more personalized.

Machine learning can be broadly categorized into three types:

- **Supervised Learning:** In this type, the model is trained using labeled data. This means that each input is paired with the correct output, allowing the algorithm to learn from the examples. For instance, a supervised learning model trained on thousands of images of cats and dogs will eventually learn to classify new images as either cats or dogs based on what it has learned.

- **Unsupervised Learning:** In unsupervised learning, the data used to train the model is not labeled. The model must figure out patterns and relationships within the data on its own. This is useful for tasks such as clustering, where the goal is to group similar data points, even if those groups are not predefined.

- **Reinforcement Learning:** This type of learning is inspired by how humans and animals learn from their environment. In reinforcement learning, the model is trained to make a series of decisions by receiving feedback in the form of rewards or penalties. For example, a reinforcement learning algorithm might be used to train a robot to navigate a maze, where each correct move brings it closer to the goal and earns a reward.

Applications of Machine Learning

Machine learning has a wide range of applications across various industries. Some typical applications include:

1. Recommendation Systems: Streaming services like Netflix and Spotify use machine learning to recommend movies or songs based on your viewing or listening history.

2. Fraud Detection: Financial institutions use machine learning algorithms to detect fraudulent transactions by analyzing patterns in transaction data.

3. Medical Diagnostics: Machine learning is being used to analyze medical images and data to diagnose diseases like cancer at an early stage.

4. Autonomous Vehicles: Self-driving cars rely heavily on machine learning to navigate, recognize objects, and make driving decisions based on real-time data.

What is Deep Learning?

Deep learning is a more advanced subset of machine learning that is modeled after the human brain's neural networks. The term "deep" refers to the multiple layers of artificial neurons (also called nodes) that process data in a hierarchy of increasing complexity. While traditional machine learning relies on structured data and shallow learning models, deep learning can handle unstructured data like images, audio, and text.

Deep learning has become a game-changer for AI, especially in tasks that require understanding complex patterns, such as image recognition, natural language processing (NLP), and voice recognition. One of the significant differences between deep learning and traditional machine learning is that deep learning models do not require feature engineering. In traditional machine learning, data scientists often need to manually define the features or characteristics that the model should focus on. Deep learning models, on the other hand, automatically identify the most relevant features from raw data during the training process.

How Deep Learning Works: Neural Networks

At the heart of deep learning are neural networks. These are algorithms inspired by the structure of the human brain, consisting of layers of interconnected nodes (neurons). Each neuron processes input and transmits the output to the next layer in the network. The deeper the network (i.e., the more layers of neurons it has), the more complex the patterns it can recognize.

Here's a breakdown of how a neural network works:

- **Input Layer:** The first layer receives raw data (e.g., an image, a piece of text, or numerical data). Each neuron in this layer processes a small piece of information from the input.

- **Hidden Layers:** These are the layers where the actual learning takes place. Each neuron in a hidden layer takes inputs from the previous layer, performs a mathematical transformation (called an activation function), and passes the result to the next layer. The network adjusts the weights of connections between neurons to improve the accuracy of its predictions.

- **Output Layer:** The final layer produces the result or prediction. For example, in an image recognition task, the output could be a label identifying whether the image contains a dog or a cat.

The learning process involves adjusting the weights of connections between neurons to minimize the difference between the predicted output and the actual output. This is done through a process called backpropagation, which allows the network to learn from its mistakes by tweaking the weights after each prediction.

Critical Concepts in Deep Learning

1. Convolutional Neural Networks (CNNs): These are specialized neural networks designed for tasks like image and video recognition. CNNs are highly effective at identifying patterns in visual data because they can process pixel information in small chunks, making them extremely good at recognizing objects and faces in images.

2. Recurrent Neural Networks (RNNs): RNNs are designed to handle sequential data, making them ideal for tasks like speech recognition

and language translation. Unlike traditional neural networks, RNNs have connections that allow information to persist across steps, which means they can remember information from previous inputs and use it to inform future predictions.

3. Transfer Learning: This technique adapts a deep learning model trained on one task to perform a different but related task. This can save a lot of time and computational resources, as the model doesn't need to be retrained from scratch.

4. Generative Adversarial Networks (GANs): GANs consist of two neural networks that compete against each other. One network (the generator) creates new data, while the other network (the discriminator) tries to determine whether the data is accurate or generated. GANs have been used to create realistic images, videos, and even music.

Applications of Deep Learning

Deep learning is revolutionizing many industries by pushing the boundaries of what AI can achieve. Some notable applications include:

1. Autonomous Vehicles: Deep learning is critical to the development of self-driving cars. It enables vehicles to recognize objects, pedestrians, and road signs, allowing them to navigate safely.

2. Healthcare: Deep learning is being used to analyze medical images, such as X-rays and MRIs, to detect diseases like cancer. It's also being used in drug discovery and personalized medicine.

3. Natural Language Processing (NLP): Virtual assistants like Google Assistant and Siri use deep learning to understand and respond to spoken language. Deep learning also powers machine translation

systems like Google Translate, allowing it to handle complex languages and nuances in meaning.

4. Entertainment: Deep learning algorithms are used in applications like Netflix's recommendation engine, which suggests content based on viewing habits. It's also used in video game development to create more realistic environments and smarter in-game characters.

Machine Learning vs. Deep Learning: What's the Difference?

While machine learning and deep learning are related, there are key differences:

1. Data Requirements: Machine learning algorithms typically require structured data (e.g., tables of numbers or text). Deep learning, on the other hand, can handle unstructured data, like images, audio, and raw text. This is why deep learning has been so successful in areas like image recognition and natural language processing.

2. Feature Engineering: In traditional machine learning, humans define the features that the algorithm should focus on (for example, pixel intensity in an image or word frequency in a text document). Deep learning models automatically learn these features from the data, making them more powerful but also more resource intensive.

3. Model Complexity: Deep learning models are typically much more complex than machine learning models, with many more parameters to optimize. This complexity allows them to solve more challenging problems, but it also means they require more computational power and data to train effectively.

Neural Networks and Their Role in AI

Neural networks form the foundation of many modern advancements in artificial intelligence (AI). These networks, inspired by the structure and function of the human brain, are the driving force behind some of the most impressive AI achievements, from image recognition to natural language processing and even autonomous systems. To understand their role in AI, it's essential to explore how they work, their evolution, and their impact on various industries.

What Are Neural Networks?

At their core, neural networks are computing systems designed to recognize patterns. They are composed of layers of interconnected nodes, also called neurons, much like the neurons in the human brain. Each neuron processes input data and applies an activation function to determine its output, which is then passed on to the next layer. The network's ability to learn from data comes from adjusting the connections (or weights) between neurons during training, much like how the human brain strengthens or weakens synapses based on learning experiences.

A typical neural network consists of three types of layers:

1. **Input Layer**: This is the layer where the network receives data. For example, if you're inputting an image, each pixel's value would be represented in the input layer.

2. **Hidden Layers**: These layers perform complex transformations of the input data. The more hidden layers a neural network has, the more profound and complex the transformations it can make, which is why

networks with many hidden layers are referred to as "deep" neural networks.

3. **Output Layer**: This is where the final predictions or classifications are made. For instance, if the network is designed to recognize animals in pictures, the output layer will indicate whether the image contains a dog, cat, or another animal.

The beauty of neural networks lies in their ability to learn from data. By adjusting the weights of the connections between neurons, neural networks can "learn" the patterns in the data and use this knowledge to make predictions or decisions.

How Neural Networks Learn

Neural networks learn through a process called **backpropagation**. During training, the network makes predictions based on input data, and the accuracy of these predictions is measured against the actual outcomes. The difference between the prediction and the actual result is calculated as an error. The network then uses this error to adjust the weights of the connections between neurons, improving its predictions over time.

For example, in a neural network trained to recognize handwritten digits, the network will make an initial prediction for each image of a digit, such as '7'7'. If the network incorrectly predicts that the image contains a '3'3' instead of a '7"7', the error is used to adjust the weights so that the next prediction is more accurate. This process is repeated thousands or even millions of times until the network can recognize digits with a high degree of accuracy.

This ability to learn from errors makes neural networks incredibly powerful and versatile. Unlike traditional algorithms that require explicit programming for every task, neural networks can adapt to new data and improve their performance through training.

Types of Neural Networks

Neural networks come in various forms, each suited to specific types of tasks. Some of the most used neural networks include:

1. **Feedforward Neural Networks (FNNs)**: This is the most basic type of neural network, where data moves in one direction from the input layer to the output layer without looping back. FNNs are used in tasks like image recognition and simple classification problems.

2. **Convolutional Neural Networks (CNNs)**: CNNs are primarily used for processing structured grid data like images. They are highly effective for tasks like image classification, object detection, and facial recognition because they can automatically detect features such as edges, textures, and shapes without manual intervention. CNNs have revolutionized the field of computer vision.

3. **Recurrent Neural Networks (RNNs)**: Unlike FNNs, RNNs can handle sequential data because they allow information to persist through loops in the network. This makes RNNs ideal for tasks like time-series prediction, language modeling, and speech recognition, where the order of the data matters.

4. **Long-Short-Term Memory Networks (LSTMs)**: A specialized form of RNNs, LSTMs are designed to overcome the limitations of standard RNNs by better handling long-range dependencies. They are widely used in tasks like machine translation, speech synthesis, and natural language processing.

5. **Generative Adversarial Networks (GANs)**: GANs consist of two neural network generators and a discriminator that compete against each other. The generator creates fake data, and the discriminator tries to distinguish between real and fake data. This competition leads to highly realistic data generation, which has been used in fields like image synthesis, video generation, and even deepfake creation.

The Role of Neural Networks in AI

Neural networks are responsible for many of the groundbreaking advancements in AI over the past decade. Their ability to process massive amounts of data, identify complex patterns, and improve performance through learning has made them a cornerstone of AI research and applications. Here are a few key areas where neural networks have had a profound impact:

1. **Image and Video Recognition**: Neural networks, particularly CNNs, are widely used in image and video recognition tasks. For example, Facebook uses CNNs to automatically tag people in photos, while Google Photos uses similar technology to categorize images based on their content. Neural networks have also been used to create deepfake videos, demonstrating their ability to generate highly realistic images and videos.

2. **Natural Language Processing (NLP)**: Neural networks have transformed the field of NLP, enabling machines to understand, interpret, and generate human language. Technologies like virtual assistants (Siri, Alexa), machine translation (Google Translate), and chatbots all rely on neural networks to process and generate language. LSTMs and transformers have been particularly effective in improving machine translation and language generation tasks.

3. **Autonomous Vehicles**: Self-driving cars rely heavily on neural networks to process sensor data and make real-time decisions. Neural networks analyze input from cameras, radar, and lidar to identify obstacles, predict traffic patterns, and navigate roads safely. Companies like Tesla and Waymo are at the forefront of this technology, using neural networks to improve the safety and reliability of autonomous vehicles.

4. **Healthcare and Diagnostics**: Neural networks are making significant strides in healthcare, particularly in medical imaging and diagnostics. For instance, neural networks can analyze medical scans to detect diseases like cancer, often with greater accuracy than human doctors. AI-driven diagnostics are becoming an essential tool for radiologists, helping them identify tumors and other abnormalities in images with high precision.

5. **Fraud Detection and Cybersecurity**: In finance and cybersecurity, neural networks detect fraudulent activities by analyzing transaction patterns and identifying anomalies. Banks and financial institutions use neural networks to prevent credit card fraud, while cybersecurity firms leverage them to identify potential threats and vulnerabilities in real-time.

The Future of Neural Networks

1. The role of neural networks in AI is set to expand even further with advancements in quantum computing. Quantum neural networks, which combine the principles of quantum mechanics with traditional neural networks, have the potential to process information at speeds that are currently unimaginable. These networks could solve problems that are too complex for classical neural networks, opening new

possibilities in fields like cryptography, materials science, and even drug discovery.

2. Additionally, as neural networks continue to evolve, they will likely play an essential role in achieving Artificial General Intelligence (AGI), the ability of a machine to perform any intellectual task that a human can do. While current AI systems excel at narrow tasks, the development of more sophisticated neural networks could bring us closer to machines with human-like cognitive abilities.

THE EVOLUTION OF PRIVACY IN THE DIGITAL AGE

The Rise of Corporate and Government Surveillance

In the digital age, the line between privacy and surveillance has become increasingly blurred. Both corporations and governments are now able to gather vast amounts of personal data, often without users' explicit consent.

Corporate Surveillance:

Corporations collect personal data in ways that many people are not even aware of. Every time you use a website, interact with social media, or shop online, companies are gathering information about you. This data is not only used to improve services or provide personalized advertisements, but it is also sold to third-party companies. These companies build detailed profiles of individuals, tracking their purchasing behavior and interests and even predicting future actions. The rise of Big Data has allowed corporations to monetize personal data, turning it into a commodity that fuels business growth and advertising.

What many people don't realize is how deep this surveillance goes. Companies use cookies, trackers, and even facial recognition software to follow users across platforms. The more sophisticated the technology becomes, the more personal and granular the data collected. This data collection extends beyond just shopping habits. For example, health apps and wearables track your fitness levels, heart rate, and sleep patterns, and in many cases, this data is shared with third-party entities. This kind of surveillance raises ethical questions about how much control individuals have over their data.

Moreover, the power imbalance between corporations and individuals continues to grow as companies use this data to manipulate consumers. By targeting users with specific content, advertisements, or information, corporations can influence decisions from what products people buy to how they vote. The fact that this process is often invisible makes it even more concerning, as users are frequently unaware that corporate interests are shaping their behavior.

Government Surveillance:

Government surveillance has also seen exponential growth, especially in the wake of global events that have led to increased national security concerns. Programs like PRISM, exposed by Edward Snowden, revealed the extent to which government agencies, such as the NSA, gather data from private citizens without their knowledge. The justification often provided for this surveillance is the need to prevent terrorism, but it has led to the erosion of personal freedoms and privacy rights.

Governments worldwide now have access to advanced technologies that enable mass surveillance. This includes monitoring phone calls, emails, online browsing histories, and even personal social media interactions. Governments can track individuals ' movements using location data from smartphones or surveillance cameras placed in public spaces. These practices raise questions about the balance between security and civil liberties as governments continue to increase their surveillance capabilities under the guise of national security.

One of the most significant concerns with government surveillance is the lack of transparency. While citizens are monitored, they often have no idea what data is being collected or how it is being used. This leads to a fundamental breakdown of trust between governments and the public. People are left wondering whether their data is being used for legitimate purposes or if it could be exploited for political or social control.

The Intersection of Corporate and Government Surveillance:

In some cases, the lines between corporate and government surveillance overlap. Governments often rely on data from private companies to carry out their surveillance activities. For example, law enforcement agencies may request user data from technology companies like Google or Facebook to investigate crimes. In many cases, these companies comply, handing over data without notifying users. This creates a complex web where personal information is shared between corporations and government entities, often without the explicit consent of the individual.

As AI technology advances, the capabilities of both corporate and government surveillance systems are likely to grow even further. Facial recognition, for instance, is increasingly being used in both the private and public sectors to track individuals' movements and behaviors. AI systems can analyze large sets of data to predict criminal activity or identify potential threats. Still, these systems also come with the risk of bias and errors, which can disproportionately affect marginalized communities.

Addressing the Growing Surveillance State:

To combat the risks posed by unchecked surveillance, there is a growing push for stronger privacy laws and regulations. In Europe, the General Data Protection Regulation (GDPR) has set a global standard for how personal data should be handled. GDPR gives individuals more control over their data and holds corporations accountable for how they collect and use it. Similar efforts are underway in other countries to curb the power of both corporations and governments to surveil their citizens.

At the same time, privacy advocates are urging individuals to take matters into their own hands by using privacy-enhancing tools like virtual private networks (VPNs), encrypted messaging apps, and secure browsers. These tools can help protect personal data from being collected and monitored by third parties, giving individuals a greater sense of control over their online privacy.

QUANTUM COMPUTING

CHALLENGES OF DIGITAL PRIVACY IN THE ERA OF SOCIAL MEDIA

In today's world, social media platforms such as Facebook, Instagram, Twitter, TikTok, and others have become deeply intertwined with our daily lives. They offer a way to stay connected, share moments, and express opinions, but they also present severe challenges to our privacy. While these platforms provide convenience and entertainment, the way they handle user data raises significant privacy concerns.

1. The Collection and Sale of Personal Data

One of the primary challenges of digital privacy in social media is the extensive collection and sale of user data. Social media platforms track almost every interaction a user has on their platforms, from the posts they like to the links they click. This data is precious to advertisers, as it helps them target users with personalized ads. For example, after picking a post about hiking, a user might start seeing ads for outdoor gear.

While this may seem harmless, the real issue is the sheer amount of data being collected. Social media platforms track far more than just the content you engage with. Thanks to cookies and embedded social media buttons, they can collect data about your location, browsing habits, friends list, private messages, and even your activity on other websites.

This information is then often sold to third-party companies or used to create detailed profiles about users. These profiles allow advertisers and other organizations to manipulate your online experience in subtle ways, often without your knowledge. For example, you might be shown certain political ads or posts that align with the platform's perception of your beliefs based on your data, which could shape your views or decisions.

2. Lack of Control Over Data

Another significant challenge is the lack of control users have over their data. Most users have little knowledge of what happens to their data once they share it on social media platforms. Even if you adjust your privacy settings to limit who can see your posts, the platform itself still has access to that information and can use it as it sees fit.

Additionally, many social media platforms make it difficult for users to delete their data. Even after deleting a post or deactivating an account, some platforms retain the data for an extended period. In some cases, they continue to use it for advertising or data analysis, which leaves users with little ability to erase their digital footprint.

3. Data Breaches and Hacking

Social media platforms are also prime targets for hackers because of the vast amount of personal data they store. Data breaches are becoming more common, and when they happen, users' personal information can be exposed to criminals who can use it for identity theft, fraud, or other malicious activities.

For example, in 2018, Facebook experienced a significant data breach, during which hackers gained access to the personal information of nearly 50 million users. Information such as email addresses, phone numbers, and even details about users' friends and contacts were exposed. Incidents like this highlight the vulnerabilities in social media platforms and the risks associated with sharing personal information online.

4. Privacy Settings and User Awareness

Most social media platforms offer privacy settings that allow users to control who can see their posts, who can contact them, and what information they want to share publicly. However, these settings can be confusing or difficult for many users to navigate. As a result, many people do not fully utilize these features, leaving their information more exposed than they realize.

For example, a user might think they are only sharing a post with their friends. Still, due to complicated privacy settings or default settings that favor public sharing, the post could be visible to a much larger audience. Additionally, privacy policies are often written in legal language that is difficult for the average user to understand, making it harder for people to make informed decisions about how their data is being used.

5. Third-party apps and Data Sharing

Many social media platforms allow third-party apps to connect to their systems. These apps might offer games, quizzes, or additional features that enhance the user experience. However, when users grant these third-party apps access, they often provide permission to gather their data, sometimes even the data of their friends.

For example, the infamous Cambridge Analytica scandal showed how a third-party app on Facebook collected data from millions of users without their explicit consent. This data was then used to target political ads and significantly influence voter behavior. The challenge here is that users often do not realize how much data third-party apps can access or how that data might be used.

6. Social Media Algorithms and Manipulation

Social media platforms use complex algorithms to curate what users see in their feeds. These algorithms prioritize content that is likely to keep users engaged, which often means promoting posts that generate strong emotional reactions. However, these algorithms can also be used to manipulate what information users see, which has profound implications for privacy and freedom of thought.

For example, if a user frequently interacts with content on a particular political issue, the platform may show them more posts and ads related to that issue, reinforcing their views. This creates an "echo chamber" where users are only exposed to information that aligns with their current beliefs, limiting diverse perspectives and possibly influencing their decisions in ways they might not realize.

Furthermore, algorithms can inadvertently expose personal information. For example, people can be suggested as "friends" based on data analysis of shared contacts or browsing behaviors, revealing personal connections that users may not have intended to share publicly.

7. The Impact on Mental Health and Privacy

Social media can also have a significant impact on mental health, which ties into privacy concerns. Constantly comparing oneself to others based on curated social media profiles can lead to anxiety, depression, and feelings of inadequacy. Moreover, the fear of missing out (FOMO) often pushes users to overshare personal details about their lives, further exposing them to privacy risks.

In some cases, users might feel pressured to present a "perfect" version of their lives online, sharing intimate details in a way that opens them up to judgment or even cyberbullying. This overexposure can lead to long-term effects on both mental well-being and personal privacy.

How AI and Quantum Computing Affect Privacy Protection

As technology progresses, both artificial intelligence (AI) and quantum computing are shaping the future of privacy protection, offering new opportunities but also posing severe challenges. These two revolutionary technologies have a profound impact on how data is handled, shared, and protected, transforming the digital landscape in unprecedented ways.

1. The Role of AI in Privacy Protection

Artificial intelligence is rapidly becoming a critical tool in managing privacy and security. Its capability to process and analyze vast amounts of data in real-time makes it both a protector of personal privacy and a potential risk to it.

AI enhances security systems in various ways. One key benefit of AI in privacy protection is its ability to monitor and detect unusual activities that could signal a cyberattack or data breach. AI-powered algorithms can track patterns of normal data usage and instantly flag any irregularities. This allows companies to respond quickly to potential threats, reducing the chance of significant data leaks. For example, AI can be used to detect and stop phishing attempts, malware attacks, and unauthorized access to sensitive information.

Moreover, AI can help companies anonymize data. When personal data is collected, AI systems can remove identifiable information, making it less vulnerable to breaches. This process, known as data anonymization, ensures that even if the data is accessed illegally, it cannot easily be traced back to an individual.

However, AI can also invade privacy. One of the most common uses of AI is to gather data about individuals, often without them even realizing it. AI systems are designed to collect and analyze data to predict user behavior, preferences, and habits. For instance, social media platforms and search engines use AI to track your activities, what you search for, and the types of content you interact with. This data is then used to show you personalized advertisements or suggest products and services.

Facial recognition technology is another example of how AI can pose a risk to privacy. AI-driven facial recognition systems are increasingly being used by governments, corporations, and even law enforcement agencies. These systems can scan and identify individuals in public spaces, raising concerns about constant surveillance and the erosion of personal privacy. People's images and activities are being monitored, often without their explicit consent, which has sparked a growing debate about the ethical use of AI in surveillance.

Additionally, the massive amounts of data collected by AI systems are stored and processed by companies, making it a potential target for cybercriminals. If these systems are not adequately secured, they can become an entry point for data breaches, leading to the exposure of susceptible personal information.

2. Quantum Computing: A Double-Edged Sword for Privacy

Quantum computing represents a dramatic leap forward in processing power, but with this comes both great potential for enhancing privacy and significant risks.

One of the biggest concerns about quantum computing is its ability to break traditional encryption methods. Currently, most online communications, financial transactions, and personal data are protected by encryption algorithms that would take classical computers thousands or even millions of years to crack. However, quantum computers, with their immense processing capabilities, could break these encryption codes in a matter of seconds.

This raises a critical concern for privacy protection. If quantum computers become widely accessible, they could be used to decrypt sensitive information, such as credit card details, medical records, and confidential communications. The risk of such decryption would put personal data, previously considered secure, at significant risk. Hackers, state actors, or other malicious entities with access to quantum computing power could access and exploit vast amounts of sensitive information. This threat has already led to increased research into quantum-resistant encryption methods to safeguard data for the future.

Despite its potential risks, quantum computing also offers innovative solutions to enhance privacy protection. One of the most promising applications is **quantum encryption**, particularly **Quantum Key Distribution (QKD)**. This method uses the principles of quantum mechanics to create secure encryption keys that cannot be intercepted or hacked without detection. In quantum mechanics, any attempt to observe or tamper with the data changes its state, alerting the parties involved.

This makes QKD virtually unhackable, providing a far more secure method of data transmission than is possible today.

In addition, quantum computing can improve the efficiency of data anonymization techniques. It can be used to create advanced algorithms that scramble and de-identify personal information to a level that would be nearly impossible for traditional computers to break. This can significantly reduce the risk of data breaches and identity theft.

Furthermore, as quantum computing continues to evolve, it may help develop new standards for cybersecurity that are much more robust than current systems. With quantum computers, it is possible to create systems that protect not just individual pieces of data but entire networks, offering a higher level of security for both personal and organizational data.

3. AI and Quantum Computing Working Together

While AI and quantum computing each pose individual challenges and opportunities for privacy, together, they have the potential to redefine how privacy is managed in the digital world.

Quantum AI:

One area of research that is gaining attention is the intersection of AI and quantum computing, known as *Quantum AI.* Quantum computers can accelerate the learning process of AI systems by processing vast amounts of data more efficiently. This could lead to AI systems that are even more advanced and capable of understanding and predicting human behavior with greater accuracy. However, this also amplifies privacy concerns, as these systems could collect and analyze more personal data than ever before, with fewer restrictions.

Quantum AI could enhance privacy protection. By combining the power of quantum computing with AI, systems that detect and neutralize cyber threats in real time could be created, preventing breaches before they happen. These systems could also manage and anonymize data at a scale far beyond what current technologies can achieve, making personal information much safer.

The Rise of Quantum Computing

Quantum computing is one of the most exciting technological advancements of the 21st century. It promises to revolutionize the way we solve complex problems, enhance data security, and handle large-scale computations. But before we explore its future potential, let's break down what quantum computing is and how it differs from the classical computers we use today.

What is Quantum Computing? The Basics

Quantum computing is a new and advanced type of computing that uses the principles of quantum mechanics, a field in physics that deals with the smallest particles in the universe, such as atoms and photons. While this might sound complicated, the main idea behind quantum computing is to solve problems much faster than traditional computers.

Traditional computers, also known as *classical computers*, store and process information using bits. A bit can either be a **0 or** a **1**, which means that classical computers perform calculations one step at a time by switching between these two values.

In contrast, quantum computers use quantum bits, or qubits, which can be both 0 and **1** at the same time due to a particular property called *superposition*. This allows quantum computers to perform multiple calculations at once, making them much more potent for specific tasks.

Superposition

Superposition is one of the key ideas in quantum computing. Imagine flipping a coin. Typically, a coin will land on either heads or tails (like a classical bit being 0 or 1). But in the world of quantum mechanics, the coin can exist in both heads and tails at the same time until you check it. In quantum computing, qubits can hold both 0 and 1 simultaneously, enabling quantum computers to solve problems much faster.

Entanglement

Another unique feature of quantum computing is **entanglement**. This means that two or more qubits can be linked together in such a way that the state of one qubit instantly affects the state of the other, even if they are far apart. This can be compared to a pair of twins who somehow know what the other is thinking, no matter how far apart they are. Entanglement allows quantum computers to work more efficiently by connecting qubits in ways that classical computers cannot.

Quantum Gates

In classical computing, operations are performed using logic gates that manipulate bits. Quantum computing uses **quantum gates to** manipulate qubits. These gates control the superposition and entanglement of qubits, allowing the quantum computer to perform complex calculations with greater efficiency.

Why Does Quantum Computing Matter?

Quantum computing is critical because it has the potential to solve problems that are currently impossible for classical computers to handle. For example:

- **Simulating Molecules**: Quantum computers could help scientists model molecules and chemical reactions, which would significantly advance fields like drug discovery and materials science.

- **Optimization Problems**: Companies could use quantum computing to optimize supply chains, improve logistics, or even design more efficient energy systems.

- **Cryptography**: Quantum computing may be able to break many of the encryption methods we use today, but it also offers new ways to secure data, making communications more secure.

BINARY CODE

QUANTUM ALGORITHMS: A GAME-CHANGER FOR DATA SECURITY

Quantum algorithms are at the heart of what makes quantum computing so powerful and different from classical computing. These algorithms take advantage of the unique properties of qubits, such as *superposition and entanglement*, to perform tasks much faster than classical algorithms ever could. In the context of data security, quantum algorithms have the potential to either disrupt or revolutionize the way we protect information.

One of the most well-known quantum algorithms is **Shor's Algorithm**. Shor's Algorithm is designed to factor large numbers incredibly fast. Why is this important? Current encryption systems, like RSA, rely on the difficulty of factoring large numbers into their prime factors. Classical computers take an extremely long time to factor such numbers, which is why RSA encryption is secure today. However, quantum computers, using Shor's Algorithm, can factor these numbers in a fraction of the time, making classical encryption methods vulnerable.

For example, RSA encryption might use a 2048-bit number (a number with 617 digits) to generate a public and private key. Breaking this encryption with a classical computer would take billions of years, but a quantum computer running Shor's Algorithm could do it in hours or even minutes. This means that all current encryption methods, including those used to secure online banking, emails, and confidential government data, could become ineffective as quantum computing technology advances.

This is why quantum algorithms are seen as both a threat and an opportunity in the field of data security. If malicious actors gain access to a quantum computer with Shor's Algorithm, they could break through today's most secure encryption systems, potentially exposing sensitive data on a massive scale.

However, it's not all bad news. Quantum computing also offers *quantum-safe solutions* to this problem. One of the most promising developments is Quantum Key Distribution (QKD), a technique that uses the principles of quantum mechanics to create unbreakable encryption keys.

Here's how it works: In QKD, encryption keys are transmitted in the form of quantum bits. If someone tries to intercept or eavesdrop on these keys, the quantum state of the qubits would be disturbed, making it impossible for the attacker to capture the key without being detected. This is because, in quantum mechanics, the mere act of observing or measuring a quantum system alters its state. As a result, QKD provides a secure way to distribute encryption keys that are immune to both classical and quantum attacks.

Grover's Algorithm is another important quantum algorithm that impacts data security. While Shor's Algorithm threatens encryption by solving the factoring problem faster, Grover's Algorithm can search through large datasets more efficiently than classical algorithms. This has significant implications for cracking symmetric encryption, such as the widely used AES (Advanced Encryption Standard). Grover's Algorithm can reduce the time it takes to brute-force a key search by half. While this doesn't completely break encryption like Shor's Algorithm, it does make current symmetric encryption less secure, as it would require doubling the key length to maintain the same level of security.

In response to these developments, cybersecurity experts and cryptographers are now focusing on post-quantum cryptography. This refers to encryption algorithms designed to be secure against attacks from both classical and quantum computers. Several promising post-quantum algorithms are being developed, but it will take time for them to be thoroughly tested and implemented on a wide scale.

At the same time, quantum computing's ability to solve certain types of problems more efficiently than classical computers also have positive applications for data security. For example, quantum algorithms can be used to develop more robust encryption systems by creating encryption methods that classical computers cannot break. Quantum-based encryption systems, such as lattice-based cryptography and hash-based signatures, are among the solutions being explored to develop quantum-resistant security.

In the long run, quantum algorithms will likely reshape the field of cryptography and data security, forcing governments, businesses, and individuals to adopt new, more secure encryption techniques. As quantum computers become more powerful, we must transition from today's vulnerable encryption systems to quantum-safe solutions that can withstand the computational capabilities of the future.

Future Implications of Quantum Computing for Cybersecurity

Quantum computing will have a transformative effect on cybersecurity, both as a threat and as a tool for enhanced protection. As we move toward a quantum-powered future, here are several critical implications:

1. Breaking Traditional Encryption Methods

Quantum computing's ability to break traditional encryption methods poses one of the most significant risks. Most encryption techniques, such as RSA and ECC (Elliptic Curve Cryptography), rely on the difficulty of factoring large numbers, a task that classical computers struggle with, but quantum computers will excel at. With *Shor's Algorithm*, a quantum computer could factor large numbers exponentially faster than any classical machine, rendering current encryption standards obsolete. This means that sensitive information, whether financial, medical, or governmental, could be vulnerable to quantum-based decryption.

2. The Need for Post-Quantum Cryptography

The rise of quantum computers has driven an urgent need for new cryptographic techniques known as post-quantum cryptography. These new encryption methods are designed to withstand attacks from quantum computers. Organizations and governments are already working on developing and testing algorithms that can protect data, even in the age of quantum computing. Soon, we will see a shift toward integrating these quantum-resistant algorithms into existing cybersecurity frameworks to ensure that sensitive data remains protected against quantum threats.

3. Enhancing Threat Detection and Prevention

While quantum computing poses significant challenges, it also offers new solutions. Quantum computers could significantly improve cybersecurity by enhancing threat detection and prevention. By processing vast amounts of data simultaneously, quantum-powered systems can identify vulnerabilities and cyberattacks in real time. For example, AI and machine learning algorithms can be integrated into quantum systems to analyze cybersecurity data faster and more accurately, detecting anomalies and potential threats before they escalate into full-blown attacks.

4. Quantum Encryption as a Defensive Tool

In addition to being a threat, quantum computing provides a defensive tool through quantum encryption, which includes techniques like Quantum Key Distribution *(QKD)*. QKD uses the laws of quantum mechanics to exchange cryptographic keys between parties securely. If any attempt is made to intercept the key, the quantum state of the particles will change, immediately alerting both parties. This makes QKD virtually unbreakable, providing a highly secure method of communication for sensitive information. Governments, financial institutions, and businesses dealing with highly confidential data will likely be among the first to adopt quantum encryption to safeguard their communications.

5. Quantum Blockchain: A New Frontier for Security

Blockchain technology, which underpins cryptocurrencies like Bitcoin, is already considered secure, but quantum computing could introduce new vulnerabilities by breaking the cryptographic algorithms that protect blockchain systems. However, researchers are also exploring the development of quantum blockchain, a new type of blockchain that leverages quantum computing's unique capabilities to enhance security. Quantum blockchain could ensure faster processing, more secure transactions, and more excellent protection against quantum threats, paving the way for the next generation of secure digital transactions.

6. Quantum-Resistant Cloud Solutions

Cloud services, which store massive amounts of sensitive data, are particularly vulnerable to quantum threats. To address this, cloud service providers are starting to explore quantum-resistant solutions. These solutions aim to protect data stored in the cloud by using post-quantum cryptographic algorithms and quantum encryption. Companies will need to adopt these technologies to ensure their cloud environments are safe from quantum-based attacks.

7. The Arms Race in Quantum Cybersecurity

There is growing concern that as quantum computing develops, there will be an arms race in cybersecurity between nations and cyber-criminals. Governments are investing heavily in quantum research to stay ahead in both offensive and defensive cybersecurity capabilities. Countries with quantum computing advancements may have a significant advantage in national security, espionage, and economic competition. As this arms race intensifies, we can expect to see stricter regulations, increased funding for quantum research, and a focus on quantum-enhanced defense mechanisms.

8. Challenges in Implementing Quantum Security

While quantum computing promises enhanced security features, implementing these technologies comes with its own set of challenges.

Quantum systems require sophisticated infrastructure, significant investment, and specialized knowledge. For many businesses, transitioning to quantum-resistant systems will involve significant overhauls in their cybersecurity architecture. Small and medium-sized enterprises (SMEs) may face difficulties in adopting quantum defenses due to the high costs associated with these new technologies. As quantum computing becomes more widespread, it will be critical to develop affordable and scalable solutions to make quantum cybersecurity accessible to all organizations.

9. Preparing for a Post-Quantum World

The most critical implication of quantum computing for cybersecurity is the need to start preparing now. Many experts believe that large-scale quantum computers capable of breaking existing encryption methods could be developed within the next decade. However, quantum-safe cryptographic systems need to be in place long before that happens. Governments, businesses, and individuals must begin transitioning to post-quantum cryptography to protect their data in the long term. This includes updating current security protocols, conducting risk assessments, and staying informed about the latest quantum advancements.

PART 2: INTEGRATING AI, BIOMETRIC SECURITY, AND QUANTUM COMPUTING

HUMAN-COMPUTER INTERFACE

AI IN CYBERSECURITY AND DATA PROTECTION

In today's digital world, cyber threats are becoming more advanced. Hackers and cybercriminals are constantly looking for new ways to steal information or cause damage to systems. To keep up with these threats, artificial intelligence (AI) has become an essential tool in cybersecurity. AI can help protect businesses, organizations, and individuals by detecting and stopping cyber threats faster and more effectively than traditional methods.

AI's ability to process large amounts of data, recognize patterns, and learn from experience makes it a powerful weapon in the fight against cybercrime. In this section, we'll explore how AI-driven tools are used in cybersecurity, how AI predicts and stops threats, and the role of biometric data in security systems.

AI-Driven Cybersecurity Tools

As cyber threats grow more sophisticated, traditional cybersecurity measures are no longer enough to protect organizations and individuals from attacks. Hackers are using advanced techniques, often exploiting vulnerabilities faster than security teams can respond. This is where AI-driven cybersecurity tools come into play, offering innovative solutions that make systems more intelligent, more adaptive, and better at defending against threats in real time.

AI-driven tools are changing the landscape of cybersecurity by using machine learning, data analysis, and automation to stay ahead of cybercriminals. Below, we investigate how these tools work and the key features that make them effective in the modern digital world.

Machine Learning in Cybersecurity

Machine learning (ML) is a branch of AI that enables systems to learn from data without being explicitly programmed. In the context of cybersecurity, ML allows security systems to analyze vast amounts of data, learn from previous attacks, and continuously improve their ability to detect and respond to new threats.

How It Works:

- **Data Collection and Analysis**: AI-driven tools collect data from various sources, such as network traffic, user behaviors, and system logs. The tools then analyze this data to identify patterns that indicate normal and abnormal activity.

- **Learning from Past Incidents**: Machine learning systems can remember past cyberattacks and detect similarities in new activities. For example, if a particular type of malware has been used before, the system will recognize similar attack methods in the future.

- **Adapting Over Time**: The more data AI systems analyze, the better they become at recognizing threats. As cyberattacks evolve, so do the machine learning algorithms, ensuring the system can handle emerging threats.

For instance, an AI-driven security tool might notice that a user who typically logs in from one country suddenly accesses the system from a different country at an unusual time. This abnormal behavior would raise a red flag, prompting the system to act, such as temporarily blocking access while security teams investigate further.

Automation in Cybersecurity

AI-driven tools also provide automation capabilities that significantly enhance cybersecurity efforts. Automation allows systems to perform specific tasks without human intervention, making the overall security process more efficient and reducing the time it takes to respond to threats.

Key Benefits of Automation:

1. **Speed and Efficiency**: AI-powered tools can automatically detect and neutralize threats in seconds, reducing the time it takes to respond to cyber incidents. For example, if a system detects malware, it can immediately isolate the infected files to prevent the malware from spreading, all without waiting for human approval.

2. **Handling Repetitive Tasks**: Many cybersecurity tasks, such as monitoring for phishing emails or checking for outdated software, are

repetitive and time-consuming. AI can automate these tasks, allowing human security experts to focus on more complex and high-priority issues.

3. **24/7 Protection**: Unlike humans, AI systems don't need breaks. AI-driven tools provide constant surveillance and monitoring systems 24/7 to ensure that any potential threats are identified as soon as they arise, even during non-working hours.

Automation also plays a crucial role in managing large-scale attacks, such as distributed denial-of-service (DDoS) attacks, which overwhelm a system with traffic. AI-driven tools can quickly recognize these attacks and deploy automated defenses, such as rerouting traffic or shutting down access points to prevent system overload.

Threat Detection and Anomaly Identification

AI tools excel at identifying anomalies, unusual patterns, or behaviors that deviate from normal system activity. These anomalies often serve as the first warning sign of a cyberattack. Unlike traditional systems that rely on predefined rules (such as blocking specific websites), AI-driven tools use advanced algorithms to detect even the most minor irregularities in network traffic, user behavior, or data flows.

How Anomaly Detection Works:

1. **Behavioral Analytics**: AI systems analyze user behaviors to establish what is "normal" for each user or system. For instance, the system might track how a user typically interacts with the network, such as login times, frequently accessed files, and location data. If the user suddenly starts accessing restricted areas of the system or logging in

at odd hours, AI can detect this abnormal behavior and flag it as suspicious.

2. **Real-Time Alerts**: Once an anomaly is detected, the AI system generates an alert in real-time. This enables security teams to investigate the issue immediately, potentially stopping a cyberattack before it does any damage.

3. **Self-Learning Models**: Unlike traditional security models that need constant updates, AI systems can self-learn and adapt based on the behavior patterns they observe. This reduces the need for frequent manual updates and ensures the system remains effective even as attack methods evolve.

For example, a company's system might experience a sudden increase in outbound network traffic, which could indicate that data is being stolen. An AI-driven tool would detect this anomaly and automatically raise an alert, allowing security teams to block suspicious activity before any sensitive data is lost.

AI-Powered Threat Intelligence

Threat intelligence is the process of gathering information about potential or ongoing threats to improve defense mechanisms. AI takes threat intelligence to the next level by processing massive amounts of data from multiple sources, such as known malware signatures, IP addresses linked to previous attacks, and threat reports from other organizations, and using that data to predict and prevent future attacks.

AI-Powered Threat Intelligence Capabilities:

- **Integration of Global Threat Data**: AI tools can analyze data from cybersecurity incidents around the world, helping organizations stay ahead of new and emerging threats. If a specific type of attack has been successful in one region, AI can alert other systems globally to prepare for similar tactics.

- **Proactive Defense**: Instead of waiting for an attack to happen, AI tools actively scan the environment for any signs of a potential threat. They use predictive analytics to foresee where attacks are likely to occur and take preventive measures, such as strengthening defenses around vulnerable areas.

- **Automated Updates**: AI-powered systems automatically update their threat databases in real-time. This ensures they are always equipped with the latest information about new malware, hacking tools, or vulnerabilities, allowing them to block attacks that traditional security systems might miss.

Enhancing Human Expertise with AI

While AI-driven tools are highly effective, they do not replace human cybersecurity experts. Instead, AI enhances human capabilities by providing faster data analysis, offering actionable insights, and reducing the workload of security teams.

Collaborative Approach:

1. **Augmenting Decision-Making**: AI systems can process large amounts of data much faster than humans, identifying trends or threats that might otherwise go unnoticed. However, human experts are still needed to make complex decisions based on the information AI provides. Together, they create a more robust defense system.

2. **Reducing False Positives**: One challenge in cybersecurity is false positives, where systems mistakenly flag legitimate activities as threats. AI-driven tools help reduce these by learning from past experiences, improving the accuracy of alerts, and reducing unnecessary disruptions.

3. **Assisting in Incident Response**: AI can quickly identify the scope of an attack, provide suggestions for containment, and even recommend remediation steps, helping human teams respond more effectively during a security breach.

PREDICTIVE AI IN IDENTIFYING AND STOPPING THREATS

Predictive AI is revolutionizing how we defend against cyber threats. Instead of reacting to attacks after they happen, predictive AI allows cybersecurity systems to foresee potential threats and act before any damage occurs. This proactive approach is a game-changer in the cybersecurity world, as it helps businesses and organizations stay ahead of cybercriminals who are constantly evolving their tactics.

How Predictive AI Works

Predictive AI relies on machine learning and big data to function effectively. Here's how it works in simple terms:

1. **Data Collection**: AI systems collect large amounts of data from various sources, including network traffic, user behavior, and historical cyberattacks. This data provides the system with information about everyday behavior and the characteristics of past cyber threats.

2. **Pattern Recognition**: AI uses machine learning algorithms to analyze this data and find patterns. For example, if a particular type of malware has been used in previous attacks, AI can identify the standard features of that malware and recognize it if it appears again. Similarly, AI can spot unusual behavior, such as a user trying to access sensitive information at an odd time or from an unusual location.

3. **Threat Prediction**: Once AI identifies suspicious patterns, it can predict potential threats before they escalate. For instance, if a

specific IP address or user behavior resembles that of a previous attack, AI can flag it as a risk and act. This predictive capability allows security teams to strengthen their defenses before an attack even begins.

Real-Time Monitoring and Alerts

Predictive AI works in real time, constantly monitoring network activity and analyzing data to identify threats as they emerge. It doesn't need to wait for an attack to be fully launched to recognize that something is wrong. This continuous monitoring is one of the most valuable features of AI in cybersecurity because it minimizes the time between detecting a threat and responding to it.

For example, if AI detects that someone is trying to log into a system from multiple locations at once, a common sign of a breach, it can automatically trigger an alert and block access. This real-time response is crucial in preventing hackers from gaining unauthorized access to sensitive information.

Stopping Known and Unknown Threats

One of the greatest strengths of predictive AI is its ability to handle both known and unknown threats:

1. **Known Threats**: Predictive AI is particularly effective at identifying known threats, such as malware or viruses that have been seen before. By learning from past attacks, AI can quickly recognize the signature of a familiar threat and stop it before it spreads.

2. **Unknown Threats (Zero-Day Threats)**: What makes AI even more powerful is its ability to detect unknown or "zero-day" threats, such as cyberattacks that exploit vulnerabilities that haven't been seen

before. AI can identify these by analyzing unusual patterns in behavior or network activity. For instance, if AI notices that a user is downloading a massive amount of data at an abnormal time, it can flag this behavior as suspicious, even if it doesn't match any previous attack. This capability makes predictive AI far more effective than traditional cybersecurity tools that rely only on known threats.

Learning and Adapting Over Time

Traditional cybersecurity systems often rely on fixed rules, meaning they can't adapt to new types of threats unless a human updates them. Predictive AI, on the other hand, continuously learns and improves over time. Each time it encounters a new threat, it learns from that experience and adjusts its behavior to better detect similar attacks in the future. This ability to learn and evolve makes AI-driven systems much more flexible and resilient than static, rule-based systems.

For example, suppose a specific type of phishing attack becomes more common. In that case, AI will start to recognize the patterns associated with that attack, such as the wording in the emails or the websites it directs users to. Over time, the system will become better at identifying phishing attempts, even as hackers change their tactics.

Using AI to Automate Threat Response

Another significant advantage of predictive AI is that it can automate the response to many threats. In the past, cybersecurity teams had to manually investigate every suspicious event, which could take time and lead to delayed responses. With AI, many of these processes are automated.

For instance, when AI detects a potential threat, such as unauthorized access to a network, it can automatically block the attacker's IP address, deactivate compromised user accounts, or isolate affected systems to prevent the spread of malware. By automating these actions, AI helps minimize the damage caused by cyberattacks and ensures that threats are dealt with swiftly and efficiently.

AI-Powered Threat Intelligence

Threat intelligence enhances AI's predictive power. It refers to the process of collecting and analyzing information about potential threats from various sources. This information can come from internal systems as well as external sources such as cybersecurity research, government alerts, and global databases of known threats.

AI uses this threat intelligence to stay current on the latest cyberattack techniques. By cross-referencing new information with its existing knowledge, AI can quickly recognize emerging threats. For example, suppose a new form of ransomware is spreading in a particular industry. In that case, AI can alert organizations in that sector to take precautionary measures before they become the next target.

Threat intelligence also helps AI systems adapt to specific industries. For instance, the types of threats faced by a financial institution may be different from those targeting healthcare organizations. AI can use industry-specific data to tailor its predictions and responses to each sector's unique risks.

Challenges and Future of Predictive AI in Cybersecurity

While predictive AI is a powerful tool, it's not without its challenges. One of the biggest hurdles is the sheer amount of data that needs to be processed. AI systems must sift through enormous volumes of information in real time, which requires significant computing power and advanced algorithms.

Another challenge is ensuring that AI doesn't produce too many false positives, which occur when the system flags harmless activity as a threat. If AI raises too many false alarms, security teams may become overwhelmed and miss real threats. Therefore, ongoing training and fine-tuning of AI systems are necessary to ensure accuracy.

Looking ahead, I predict AI will continue to play an increasingly important role in cybersecurity. As cyber threats become more sophisticated, AI's ability to learn, adapt, and predict attacks will be essential in keeping systems secure. Future advancements in AI, such as integrating it with quantum computing, could make these systems even more powerful, allowing them to detect threats faster and with even greater precision.

The Role of Biometrics in AI Security Systems

Biometric security, which involves using physical or behavioral traits like fingerprints, facial recognition, or voice patterns, has revolutionized how we protect sensitive data. However, as sophisticated as these systems are, they become even more powerful when combined with artificial intelligence (AI). AI enhances the security and functionality of biometric systems in several critical ways, ensuring that they are reliable, secure, and adaptable to the ever-changing landscape of cybersecurity.

Biometrics provides a unique solution to the problem of authentication, verifying that a person is who they say they are. Unlike traditional methods such as passwords, which can be forgotten or stolen, biometric data is unique to each person. This makes it difficult for hackers to forge or steal. Yet even biometric systems have limitations. For example, changes in a person's environment (such as lighting for facial recognition) or attempts to spoof the system using fake fingerprints or photos can challenge their accuracy. This is where AI plays a vital role.

AI enhances biometric systems by learning from data and improving its ability to recognize individuals more accurately over time. AI systems are trained on massive amounts of biometric data, allowing them to adapt to the nuances of each person's unique traits. For instance, in facial recognition, AI can adjust to variations in lighting, angles, or even changes in a person's appearance, such as aging or growing a beard. Similarly, voice recognition systems powered by AI can recognize a person's voice even if they are cold or there is background noise. This adaptability ensures that biometric systems remain accurate and functional in various real-world situations.

AI also plays a crucial role in making biometric systems more secure by preventing fraud. One of the most significant risks in biometric security is spoofing, where attackers try to trick the system by using fake fingerprints, photos, or recorded voices to impersonate an authorized user. AI helps to detect and stop these kinds of attacks. For example, in facial recognition systems, AI can detect subtle movements like blinking or changes in facial expression, which are nearly impossible to replicate with a photograph. In voice recognition systems, AI can analyze the quality and natural flow of speech, spotting inconsistencies that would indicate someone is using a recording rather than speaking in real-time.

The integration of AI with biometrics enhances accuracy and offers real-time monitoring and alerts. AI can continuously monitor biometric systems, identifying potential security threats or unusual behavior. If someone tries to access a system using forged biometric data, AI can detect the anomaly and immediately block the attempt, alerting security teams to the breach. This kind of proactive defense is essential in a world where cyber threats are constantly evolving.

Biometric data, while secure, raises concerns about privacy. Once your biometric data is compromised, it cannot be changed like a password. AI helps mitigate these privacy risks by encrypting biometric data and using advanced algorithms to ensure that the data is stored and managed securely. Even if attackers manage to access the data, AI-driven encryption makes it much more difficult for them to make use of it. Additionally, AI can be programmed to follow privacy regulations, ensuring that organizations handle biometric data responsibly and in line with legal standards like the GDPR.

Furthermore, AI-driven biometric systems are becoming a key component of multi-factor authentication (MFA), a security process that requires users to present two or more verification factors. Combining biometrics with other authentication methods, such as a password or a security token, enhances security. AI ensures that this combination of factors works seamlessly, reducing the chance of unauthorized access. For instance, if a biometric scan is paired with a one-time password sent to the user's phone, AI ensures that both factors are verified quickly and accurately before access is granted.

Looking ahead, the partnership between AI and biometrics will continue to drive innovations in cybersecurity. As both technologies evolve, we can expect even more advanced applications, such as using brainwave patterns or heart rhythms as biometric identifiers. AI will play a crucial role in managing and securing these new forms of biometric data, ensuring that security systems remain adaptable, accurate, and difficult to hack.

ZERO TRUST: BUILDING A PROACTIVE CYBERSECURITY FRAMEWORK

The Zero Trust model is a modern approach to cybersecurity that challenges the traditional "castle and moat" mentality. In the past, organizations assumed that if they protected the perimeter of their network with strong defenses like firewalls, everything inside the network would be safe. This is like the idea of a castle with walls protecting everything inside it. However, as cyber threats have evolved and workplaces have shifted to cloud services, mobile devices, and remote work, the perimeter has become more porous, and traditional security measures are no longer enough.

The Zero Trust model turns this idea on its head by assuming that no one, inside or outside the network, can be trusted by default. Instead, every user, device, and application must prove their legitimacy every time they attempt to access company resources. In this way, Zero Trust continuously verifies users and resources, preventing unauthorized access and minimizing risks.

Here are the core principles that define the Zero model.

Never Trust, Always Verify

At the heart of Zero Trust is the idea that you should never trust anyone automatically. Traditional models assume that once a user is inside the network, they can be trusted. However, under Zero Trust, even users who are already inside the network must be continuously verified. This applies to every action they take, from accessing a file to sending an email.

This approach mitigates the risk of internal threats and compromised accounts, as every user, even employees, contractors, and partners, must be authenticated and authorized before they can access sensitive data. Authentication doesn't happen just once when the user logs in; it is repeated for every action throughout their session.

Least Privilege Access

Zero Trust enforces the concept of least privilege access, which means that users and devices should only be granted the minimum level of access necessary to perform their tasks. For example, an employee in the marketing department shouldn't have access to the company's financial records unless it's essential for their role.

This minimizes the risk of internal threats by limiting how much damage a compromised account can do. Even if an attacker gains access to a user's credentials, their ability to cause harm is restricted by the limited permissions associated with that account.

Micro-Segmentation

A traditional network often operates as a single, large zone where users can move freely once they gain access. The Zero Trust model changes this by dividing the network into smaller, secure zones, each with its own set of security controls. This is known as micro-segmentation.

Micro-segmentation allows organizations to control how data flows between different parts of the network. For example, sensitive financial data might be stored in one segment while customer service systems are housed in another. By restricting access between these segments, Zero Trust prevents an attacker from moving laterally across the network if they manage to breach one area.

This makes it harder for cybercriminals to escalate privileges or gain access to more critical systems after an initial breach, significantly reducing the potential damage of an attack.

Multi-Factor Authentication (MFA)

One of the fundamental aspects of Zero trust is the use of Multi-Factor Authentication (MFA). MFA requires users to present multiple forms of identification to verify their identity, such as a password, a code sent to their phone, or a biometric factor like a fingerprint. This ensures that even if a user's password is stolen, unauthorized access can still be blocked.

By requiring multiple forms of verification, Zero Trust reduces the chances that a cybercriminal can successfully impersonate an authorized user. MFA is critical in today's cybersecurity landscape, where passwords alone are no longer enough to secure access.

Continuous Monitoring and Logging

In traditional security models, once a user gains access, they are typically not monitored closely. Zero Trust, on the other hand, requires continuous monitoring of user activity. Every action is logged, and abnormal behavior is flagged for immediate investigation.

Continuous monitoring ensures that if a user starts behaving suspiciously, such as attempting to access data they don't usually need to or logging in from an unusual location, the system can detect these anomalies and take corrective action. This might involve locking the account, sending an alert to the IT team, or requiring additional authentication.

Strong Device Security

The Zero Trust model verifies users and the devices they use. With more employees working remotely and using personal devices, it's essential to ensure that all devices accessing company resources meet security standards. This includes checking for up-to-date antivirus software, encryption, and secure configurations.

Zero Trust frameworks often use Endpoint Detection and Response (EDR) solutions to monitor devices constantly for signs of compromise. If a device is found to be at risk, such as running outdated software, it can be quarantined or blocked from accessing the network until the issue is resolved.

Defense in Depth

Zero Trust is not a single tool or technology but rather a comprehensive strategy that integrates multiple layers of security. This is often referred to as defense in depth, where each layer of security works together to protect the network. If one layer is compromised, the others are still in place to stop or slow down an attacker.

This layered approach involves firewalls, encryption, intrusion detection systems (IDS), antivirus programs, and behavioral analytics, all working in concert. By combining multiple layers of defense, Zero Trust creates a more resilient security posture.

Implementing Zero Trust: Practical Steps for Businesses

To successfully adopt the Zero Trust security model, businesses must take a strategic approach that integrates verification and monitoring at every stage of network access. Zero Trust, which operates on the principle of "never trust, always verify," aims to eliminate implicit Trust by requiring continuous authentication and authorization, even for users inside the network.

The first step in implementing Zero Trust is to map out all your data and resources. Businesses should identify where their most sensitive information, such as customer records, financial data, or intellectual property, is stored and understand how that data is accessed. This mapping process will highlight critical areas that require extra security, ensuring efforts are focused on protecting the most vulnerable parts of the system.

Multi-factor authentication (MFA) is a cornerstone of Zero Trust. By requiring more than just a password, such as a biometric scan or a verification code sent to a user's phone, businesses add a layer of protection that makes it harder for attackers to gain access, even if they have stolen login credentials. Enforcing MFA across all user accounts is a critical step in safeguarding data, whether employees are accessing systems from the office, home, or on the go.

Another essential component is segmenting your network. By breaking the network into smaller, secure zones, businesses can limit how far an intruder can move if they manage to breach the system. This principle, known as micro-segmentation, ensures that users can only access the parts of the network they need for their role. A finance team, for example, should not have access to marketing or IT systems. Segmentation also supports the concept of least privilege, ensuring that users only have the minimum access required to perform their jobs, reducing the risk of internal breaches.

Continuous monitoring is vital to the Zero Trust model. User activity must continuously be tracked, with systems in place to detect unusual or suspicious behavior. Businesses can use advanced analytics and behavior monitoring tools to identify when users are acting out of the ordinary, such as logging in from an unfamiliar location or attempting to access files they wouldn't usually need. Any deviations should trigger an automatic response, such as requesting additional verification or suspending access until the user's identity is confirmed.

Cloud and remote access security are also key aspects of implementing Zero Trust. With more employees working remotely, businesses need to secure cloud platforms by ensuring that all connections are encrypted and that users authenticate their identities every time they access cloud-based services. Zero Trust Network Access (ZTNA) solutions help achieve this by requiring users to pass strict identity checks before gaining access to company applications, regardless of where they are located.

Regular system updates and patching are crucial to prevent attackers from exploiting known vulnerabilities. Automated systems should be used to ensure that all software is up to date, including operating systems, applications, and any third-party tools used by the business. Vulnerability scanning tools can also help detect weak points that need immediate attention.

Lastly, businesses must invest in employee training. Employees are often the weakest link in any cybersecurity framework, and without proper education, they may fall victim to phishing attacks or other social engineering tactics. Regular training sessions should educate staff on security best practices, such as identifying suspicious emails, creating strong passwords, and understanding the importance of MFA. Encouraging a Zero Trust mindset among employees, where no one is automatically trusted, is essential for creating a secure environment.

By following these steps, businesses can effectively implement Zero Trust, ensuring their networks and data remain protected from both internal and external threats. Zero Trust is not a one-time project but an ongoing process that requires regular updates and adjustments as the threat landscape evolves.

How Quantum Computing Will Enhance Zero Trust Strategies

The evolution of cybersecurity has led to the development of increasingly sophisticated models to defend against the ever-growing threat landscape. Among these, the Zero Trust model stands as one of the most effective frameworks for protecting data and systems by shifting the focus from perimeter-based defenses to a more dynamic, internal verification model. However, as digital threats continue to evolve, and with the rise of technologies such as quantum computing, the need for more advanced cybersecurity strategies has become apparent.

Quantum computing, a technology that leverages the principles of quantum mechanics to process vast amounts of information simultaneously, has the potential to fundamentally transform how we approach cybersecurity, particularly in enhancing the Zero Trust model. As quantum technology matures, it promises to redefine encryption, authentication, threat detection, and data integrity measures, creating a much more secure digital landscape.

UNDERSTANDING THE BASICS OF
QUANTUM COMPUTING

Quantum computing differs from classical computing in that it uses qubits instead of bits. While classical computers process information in binary form (either 0 or 1), qubits can exist in both states simultaneously due to the principle of superposition. Additionally, quantum entanglement allows qubits to be linked so that changes in one qubit can instantaneously affect another, no matter the distance between them. This parallel processing capability means that quantum computers can solve complex problems and handle vast amounts of data much faster than today's most powerful supercomputers.

In the context of cybersecurity, quantum computing's potential lies in its ability to break current encryption methods and create much stronger encryption protocols that would be virtually impossible for classical computers to breach. This dual potential of breaking and securing encryption makes quantum computing crucial to the future of cybersecurity.

The Current Challenges of Zero Trust Security

The Zero Trust model which operates on the principle of "never trust, always verify, "requires continuous verification of users, devices, and network activity, regardless of whether they are inside or outside the corporate firewall. While this model addresses many of the vulnerabilities present in traditional perimeter-based defenses, it also faces challenges:

1. **Speed of Verification**: As systems grow more complex and the number of users increases, verifying access requests in real-time becomes more difficult.

2. **Data Integrity**: Ensuring that data has not been tampered with, especially as it moves across networks, is a constant concern.

3. **Threat Detection**: Classical systems can find it challenging to detect sophisticated attacks, especially ones that evolve rapidly or are targeted.

4. **Encryption Vulnerability**: Current encryption methods, such as RSA, are theoretically breakable by quantum computers in a matter of minutes or hours, posing a significant risk to data security.

Quantum computing holds the potential to address many of these challenges, thereby significantly enhancing the effectiveness of the **Zero Trust model**.

Quantum Computing's Impact on Zero Trust Strategies

1. Stronger Encryption: Quantum-Resistant Algorithms

One of the biggest threats quantum computing poses to cybersecurity is its ability to break traditional encryption methods. Today, encryption standards such as RSA (Rivest–Shamir–Adleman) and ECC (Elliptic Curve Cryptography) rely on the difficulty of factoring large prime numbers, a task that classical computers struggle with. However, Shor's algorithm, a quantum algorithm, can perform this task exponentially faster, rendering current encryption methods vulnerable.

To counteract this threat, the field of quantum-resistant encryption, or post-quantum cryptography, has emerged. These encryption algorithms are designed to be secure even against quantum attacks. In the context of the Zero Trust model, these new encryption methods will be critical for:

- **Securing Communications**: As data moves across networks and between devices, ensuring that it remains encrypted and secure is essential to Zero Trust. Quantum-resistant encryption will ensure that data remains protected, even in a world where quantum computers are a threat.

- **Protecting Stored Data**: Encrypting stored data using quantum-resistant algorithms will protect it from future quantum attacks. In a zero-trust environment, data protection must extend beyond transmission to include secure storage.

- **Quantum Key Distribution (QKD)**: One of the most promising applications of quantum computing in cybersecurity is quantum key distribution. QKD allows two parties to generate a shared, secret encryption key over a quantum channel.

If an eavesdropper attempts to intercept the key, the laws of quantum mechanics ensure that both parties are aware of the intrusion. This real-time detection and the impossibility of copying quantum data without altering it make QKD an ideal method for securing communication in a Zero-Trust architecture.

2. Enhanced Authentication through Quantum Biometrics

Biometric security, such as fingerprint recognition, facial scans, or voice identification, plays a vital role in Zero Trust strategies by providing an additional layer of authentication. However, as advanced hacking techniques and deepfake technologies become more prevalent, even biometric systems are vulnerable to attack.

Quantum computing can enhance biometric security through the development of quantum biometrics. In quantum biometrics, unique quantum states represent a user's biometric data. These quantum states are impossible to clone due to the no-cloning theorem in quantum mechanics, which prevents exact copies of unknown quantum states from being made.

Incorporating quantum biometrics into the zero-trust model could offer several benefits:

- **Unforgeable Authentication**: Quantum biometrics could make it impossible for attackers to clone or spoof a user's biometric data, ensuring that only the legitimate user can gain access to the system.

- **Continuous Verification**: Since quantum biometric data is constantly in flux, it could be used for continuous verification, a key component of Zero Trust, where user behavior is continuously monitored to detect unusual activity.

- **Faster, More Secure Access**: Quantum computing's processing power allows for faster processing of biometric data, reducing the lag in authentication while ensuring higher security standards.

3. Advanced Threat Detection and Response

One of the pillars of the **Zero Trust model** is the ability to monitor and respond to threats continuously in real-time. Quantum computing's ability to process massive amounts of data quickly and its capacity for pattern recognition can significantly improve threat detection capabilities.

Currently, AI-powered cybersecurity systems use machine learning algorithms to detect anomalies or suspicious behavior in network traffic. The processing power of classical computers limits these systems. Quantum computers, however, can:

- **Process More Data**: Quantum computers can analyze vast amounts of network data simultaneously, identifying patterns that classical systems might miss.

- **Enhance AI Models**: Quantum computing can improve machine learning models by accelerating the training process. This can lead to more accurate predictions of potential threats, allowing for proactive defenses rather than reactive responses.

- **Improve Real-Time Response**: Quantum-enhanced AI systems could detect and respond to threats in real time, enabling the immediate shutdown of unauthorized access or suspicious activity within a Zero-Trust framework.

In a zero-trust environment, where constant vigilance is required, quantum-powered threat detection systems could provide a significant edge over cyber attackers.

4. Securing the Internet of Things (IoT) with Quantum Computing

The growth of the Internet of Things (IoT) has added complexity to the Zero Trust model. With countless devices connected to networks, each device represents a potential vulnerability. Traditional security methods struggle to keep up with the sheer volume and diversity of IoT devices, making them a prime target for attackers.

Quantum computing offers solutions for securing IoT devices in several ways:

- **Quantum-Secure IoT Networks**: Quantum key distribution could secure communication between IoT devices and central servers, ensuring that the data transmitted between devices remains confidential and tamper-proof.

- **Device Authentication**: Quantum biometrics could be applied to IoT devices to ensure that only authorized devices can communicate with the network. This could prevent attackers from using compromised devices to infiltrate the network.

- **Quantum-Based Intrusion Detection**: By processing data in parallel, quantum computing could enhance IoT networks' ability to detect unusual activity or intrusions across millions of connected devices.

5. Quantum Cryptography: Securing the Future of Digital Infrastructure

The future of the Zero Trust model will heavily rely on advancements in quantum cryptography, which offers an entirely new way of securing digital infrastructure.

- **Quantum Random Number Generators (QRNGs)**: In classical cryptography, random number generators are used to create encryption keys. However, these generators can sometimes be predictable. Quantum random number generators, by contrast, use the inherent unpredictability of quantum processes to generate truly random numbers, resulting in much more secure encryption keys.

- **Quantum Secure Cloud Computing**: As cloud computing becomes increasingly integral to business operations, securing cloud environments will be crucial. Quantum computing can provide enhanced encryption methods to protect data stored in the cloud, ensuring that only verified users have access to critical business data.

CYBER AND NETWORKING

BIOMETRIC DATA AND SECURITY IN THE AGE OF AI

In today's rapidly evolving digital landscape, traditional methods of securing data are no longer enough. As cybersecurity threats become more advanced, the need for more robust, more reliable security measures grows. One such method that has emerged as a crucial tool in enhancing security is biometric data. Biometrics, the measurement of human characteristics such as fingerprints, facial features, and voice patterns, is now being used as a primary defense in protecting sensitive information. Coupled with artificial intelligence (AI), biometric systems have the potential to revolutionize how we secure data in the digital age.

Biometric security systems are already part of our daily lives. From unlocking smartphones with facial recognition to using fingerprints to access financial accounts, these technologies have made their way into both personal and business environments. However, as these systems become more prevalent, they also raise significant privacy and ethical concerns that must be addressed.

The Rise of Biometric Data as a Security Measure

The increasing reliance on digital platforms and systems for personal, professional, and financial activities has exposed individuals and organizations to a growing range of security threats. From cyberattacks to identity theft, securing data has become a critical priority across various sectors. Traditional security measures such as passwords, PINs, and security questions, though still commonly used, are proving to be inadequate in the face of more sophisticated hacking techniques. These traditional methods are vulnerable because they rely on information that can be easily guessed, stolen, or compromised through phishing or social engineering.

Biometric data has emerged as a robust alternative to these outdated methods, offering a higher level of security by using unique biological characteristics for identification. Biometric security uses an individual's physical or behavioral traits, such as fingerprints, facial features, voice patterns, and even iris scans, as authentication methods. Unlike passwords, which can be shared or forgotten, biometric traits are unique to each person and cannot be easily replicated. This makes biometric authentication systems far more secure and less prone to unauthorized access.

Why Biometrics Are More Secure

One of the main reason biometrics are considered more secure than traditional security measures is their uniqueness. Every person has distinct physical and behavioral characteristics, meaning no two people have identical fingerprints, irises, or voices. This inherent uniqueness adds a layer of protection that makes it extremely difficult for unauthorized individuals to forge or mimic biometric data. For example, a fingerprint used in a security system cannot be shared or duplicated the way a password can.

Additionally, biometric data is difficult to steal or manipulate because it is tied directly to a person's physical being. Even if hackers were to gain access to a database of biometric information, replicating that data in a form that could bypass security systems is challenging. While passwords can be stolen in bulk from unsecured databases, biometric data typically requires access to the individual's physical presence for authentication, which makes large-scale breaches less feasible.

Another key advantage is the convenience of biometric systems. Users no longer need to remember complex passwords or worry about forgetting their security credentials. With biometric authentication, a simple scan of a fingerprint, face, or retina can grant access to a device or account. This ease of use, combined with its superior security, has made biometrics an attractive solution for both individuals and organizations seeking to enhance their cybersecurity measures.

Historical Development of Biometric Security

The use of biometric data in security is not entirely new. Biometric technologies have been employed for decades in various high-security environments, such as government institutions, military bases, and airports. Early biometric systems were primarily used for fingerprint analysis, which remains one of the most used biometric methods today. In these settings, biometric data was used to authenticate individuals who needed access to restricted areas or sensitive information.

However, the use of biometric data was limited by the high cost of the technology and the complexity of implementing such systems on a large scale. For many years, only governments or large corporations could afford to deploy biometric systems due to the significant infrastructure and maintenance costs. In addition, early biometric systems were relatively slow and less accurate than they are today, which made them unsuitable for widespread use in consumer applications.

With the rapid advancement of artificial intelligence (AI) and machine learning in recent years, the capabilities of biometric systems have significantly improved. AI has allowed biometric systems to become more precise, efficient, and cost-effective, making them accessible to a wider range of users. What once was exclusive to high-security environments is now commonplace in consumer electronics. Devices such as smartphones, laptops, and even household security systems are now equipped with biometric authentication, including facial recognition and fingerprint scanners.

Consumer Adoption of Biometrics

The introduction of biometric authentication in consumer devices began to gain traction with the release of fingerprint scanners on smartphones in the early 2010s. Apple's introduction of Touch ID on the iPhone in 2013 marked a turning point for biometric security in consumer technology. The convenience and protection offered by fingerprint authentication quickly made it a popular feature among users, prompting other manufacturers to adopt similar technologies in their devices. Soon after, facial recognition technology followed Apple's Face ID, which further popularized biometrics as a mainstream security tool.

Today, millions of people around the world use biometric authentication to unlock their phones, access banking apps, and verify their identities in various online services. This widespread adoption of biometric technology has been driven by its ease of use and the growing demand for enhanced security in a digital-first world. Biometrics has become an integral part of everyday life, providing seamless security without the need for cumbersome passwords or PIN codes.

Biometric authentication has also gained traction in industries such as banking, healthcare, and e-commerce, where secure identity verification is critical. Banks, for example, have incorporated fingerprint and facial recognition into their mobile banking apps to enable customers to securely access their accounts without needing to remember passwords. In healthcare, biometrics are being used to secure access to medical records and ensure that only authorized personnel can view sensitive patient data.

Biometric Security Beyond Consumer Devices

Beyond personal devices, biometrics has also become a cornerstone of security for critical infrastructure and corporate environments. In large organizations, biometric access control systems restrict entry to secure areas and prevent unauthorized access to sensitive data. For example, employees may be required to scan their fingerprints or use facial recognition technology to enter secure facilities or access classified information on corporate networks.

Additionally, law enforcement agencies have long used biometric systems, particularly fingerprint and facial recognition databases, to identify criminals and solve cases. As these systems have improved, their ability to identify individuals based on partial or degraded biometric data has also advanced, making them indispensable tools in criminal investigations.

Moreover, biometric systems are increasingly being used in national security settings. Governments worldwide are deploying biometric technologies at border crossings and airports to streamline security checks and verify travelers' identities. These systems allow authorities to quickly authenticate individuals, reducing the chances of fraud or impersonation. In some countries, biometric passports have been introduced, embedding a digital version of the passport holder's biometric data to enhance travel security.

AI's Role in Advancing Biometric Security

Artificial intelligence has played a pivotal role in advancing the capabilities of biometric systems. AI algorithms can analyze biometric data with greater accuracy and speed than ever before, enabling biometric systems to identify and authenticate individuals quickly. For instance, AI-powered facial recognition systems can differentiate between thousands of faces in a crowd, making them ideal for use in large public spaces like airports, stadiums, and transportation hubs.

AI also enables continuous learning within biometric systems. As the system gathers more data, it can refine its ability to recognize individuals and detect anomalies. For example, AI algorithms can learn to identify a person's face even if their appearance has changed over time, such as through aging or changes in hairstyle. This adaptability ensures that biometric systems remain effective over long periods, even as users' physical characteristics change.

The integration of AI into biometric security has also enabled the development of more sophisticated multi-modal systems, which combine multiple biometric traits for authentication. For example, a system might use a combination of facial recognition, voice recognition, and fingerprint scanning to verify an individual's identity. By relying on more than one biometric trait, these systems offer enhanced security and reduce the likelihood of false positives or negatives.

While biometrics offer significant advantages, there are still challenges to their widespread adoption. One primary concern is the security and privacy of biometric data itself. Unlike a password, which can be changed if compromised, biometric data is permanent. If a person's biometric data is stolen, it cannot be easily replaced. This creates the risk that once stolen; biometric data could be used for malicious purposes for the remainder of a person's life.

Additionally, as the use of biometrics becomes more widespread, there is growing concern over how this data is being collected, stored, and shared. Governments and private organizations alike must ensure that biometric data is protected with the highest levels of security and that users are aware of how their data is being used. Implementing robust data protection laws and ensuring that organizations follow ethical standards in the use of biometrics will be crucial in addressing these concerns.

Biometric security is likely to become even more advanced with the continued integration of AI and other emerging technologies like quantum computing. Quantum computing has the potential to revolutionize biometric systems by providing unprecedented levels of encryption and processing power. With quantum-powered biometric systems, the encryption of biometric data could become virtually unbreakable, providing an additional layer of security for sensitive information.

Privacy Risks and Ethical Concerns of Biometric Data

While biometric security systems offer significant advantages in protecting sensitive information, they also introduce unique and substantial privacy risks. Unlike traditional passwords or PINs, which can be easily changed in the event of a breach, biometric data is permanent. Your fingerprint, iris scan, or facial features are immutable, meaning that if compromised, these forms of identification cannot simply be altered or updated. This permanence makes the stakes of biometric breaches far higher than those involving traditional security measures. The implications of such a breach can be severe and long-lasting, raising a series of ethical questions about how biometric data is managed, protected, and used.

Data Breaches and the Irreversibility of Biometric Data Loss

The most immediate and pressing privacy risk associated with biometrics is the possibility of a data breach. In the event of a violation, sensitive biometric information such as fingerprints or facial recognition data could be stolen. While a password or PIN can be reset, there is no way to replace a fingerprint or retina scan. This leaves individuals whose biometric data has been compromised in a vulnerable position, as that information can be used for identity theft, fraud, or unauthorized surveillance.

Moreover, biometric databases where this data is stored are prime targets for cybercriminals. These databases contain not just one piece of sensitive information but a collection of biometric data from potentially millions of individuals. If breached, the scope of the damage could be enormous.

Unlike a credit card number that can be canceled and replaced, biometric data is a lifetime identifier. Once it's out in the open, individuals cannot reclaim their privacy in the same way they can with other personal data.

Governments, corporations, and institutions that store biometric data must, therefore, implement extremely robust security measures to prevent unauthorized access. However, no system is foolproof, and the risks of data breaches are always present. The ethical question then arises: *Should organizations be allowed to collect such sensitive information if they cannot guarantee its absolute security?*

The Collection and Storage of Biometric Data

Another significant concern is the collection and storage of biometric data. Many users are unaware of the extent to which their biometric information is collected and how it is stored. For example, when individuals use facial recognition to unlock their phones or log in to apps, they may not realize that this data is often stored in a central database. In some cases, the data may even be shared with third parties, raising concerns about who has access to it and how it may be used in the future.

In addition to storage issues, there is the problem of informed consent. Many individuals do not fully understand how their biometric data is being collected, how long it is stored, and who has access to it. This lack of transparency leaves individuals vulnerable to having their data used in ways they did not agree to. For example, if a company collects facial recognition data to verify user identity, could that data later be sold or shared with law enforcement without the user's knowledge?

This concern is particularly relevant in the context of surveillance. Many governments and corporations have begun using biometric systems not only for security purposes but also for monitoring individuals. For example, some countries have implemented widespread facial recognition surveillance in public spaces, tracking individuals' movements and behaviors without their explicit consent. This raises ethical questions about the balance between security and personal privacy and the potential for abuse of power.

Ethical Concerns of Mass Surveillance

One of the most controversial uses of biometric data is its application in **mass surveillance systems**. Facial recognition technology, for instance, has been deployed by several governments around the world to monitor and track citizens in public spaces. While proponents argue that these technologies can enhance security, particularly in preventing crime or terrorism, critics warn that such systems can easily be abused.

The ethical dilemma centers on the potential for privacy invasion. With facial recognition systems, individuals can be tracked without their knowledge or consent, and this information can be used to build detailed profiles of their activities and movements. In some cases, this data can be linked to social media accounts, purchasing habits, and other personal information, creating a comprehensive dossier on individuals. This level of surveillance can infringe upon civil liberties, as individuals lose their ability to move freely without being watched.

Furthermore, the use of biometric surveillance in politically repressive regimes can lead to the targeting of specific groups or individuals, such as political dissidents, journalists, or activists. The ability to track people so precisely creates the risk that biometric data can be used as a tool of oppression, silencing voices of dissent and reducing individual freedom. These concerns call into question the ethical implications of widespread biometric surveillance and whether it is indeed justified in the name of security.

Bias in AI-Driven Biometric Systems

Another major ethical concern surrounding the use of biometric data is the presence of bias in AI-driven biometric systems. Although AI has made biometric systems faster and more accurate, they are not without flaws. AI algorithms that are trained to recognize faces, fingerprints, or voices may not perform equally well across different demographic groups, such as race, gender, or age.

Studies have shown that some facial recognition technologies have higher error rates when identifying people of color, women, and older individuals. This bias arises because the datasets used to train these algorithms are often skewed toward specific demographics usually white male faces resulting in poor performance when recognizing individuals who do not fit that profile.

The consequences of such bias can be far-reaching. For example, an AI system with built-in bias could lead to false positives or negatives in identification. In law enforcement, this could mean wrongly accusing an innocent person of a crime based on faulty facial recognition data. In a corporate setting, it could lead to the exclusion of specific individuals from services or benefits because the system fails to recognize them accurately.

Addressing bias in biometric systems requires a concerted effort to ensure that the data used to train AI algorithms is diverse and representative of the population. It also requires ongoing testing and validation to identify and correct any biases that emerge. The ethical imperative here is to ensure that biometric systems are fair and do not disproportionately impact specific groups of people.

The Ethical Debate on Consent and Control

Consent and control are crucial ethical issues when it comes to biometric data. Unlike traditional data, biometric information is deeply personal and tied directly to an individual's identity. As such, individuals should have the right to control how their biometric data is collected, stored, and used. However, in many cases, this control is either limited or non-existent.

For example, when a person uses a biometric authentication system, they may not fully understand where their data is going or how it is being protected. Additionally, once their biometric data is stored in a database, the individual often loses control over it. This raises the question of whether individuals are genuinely giving informed consent when they use biometric systems or whether they are being coerced into handing over their personal information in exchange for convenience.

Moreover, biometric data retention policies vary widely, with some organizations keeping this data indefinitely. Without strict guidelines and regulations, individuals may unknowingly allow companies or governments to hold onto their biometric information long after it is no longer needed. This lack of control over one's biometric identity is a significant ethical concern, as it leaves individuals vulnerable to privacy violations and abuse.

The Risk of Function Creep

Another important ethical issue is the risk of function creep, which is the gradual expansion of the use of biometric data beyond its original purpose. For example, a company might initially collect biometric data for secure login purposes but then begin using that data for marketing, behavioral tracking, or even surveillance without informing users. This expansion of use, often done without user consent, can result in significant privacy violations.

Function creep is particularly dangerous because it is often difficult for individuals to track how their data is being used. Once biometric data is collected, it can be repurposed for any number of uses, many of which may not align with the original intention. This lack of transparency erodes trust and increases the likelihood that biometric systems will be used in ways that harm users rather than protect them.

To prevent function creep, strong regulations and policies must be put in place to limit how biometric data can be used. Individuals should also have the right to opt out of biometric data collection or to withdraw their data once it has served its original purpose. These protections are essential for ensuring that biometric systems are used ethically and responsibly.

AI-Driven Biometric Systems for Enhanced Privacy and Security

Biometric systems have proven to be one of the most effective and convenient ways to authenticate users and protect sensitive information. When combined with artificial intelligence (AI), these systems become even more powerful, enabling faster, more accurate, and more secure authentication processes. AI-driven biometric systems can process vast amounts of data, detect subtle patterns that humans might miss, and continuously learn and adapt to new challenges in real time. This dynamic combination of biometrics and AI provides enhanced privacy and security, making it a critical tool for businesses, governments, and individuals.

Advanced Capabilities of AI in Biometrics

One of the key advantages of integrating AI with biometric systems is its ability to analyze multiple layers of data beyond what traditional biometric systems can. For instance, AI algorithms can process fingerprints, facial features, iris patterns, and even behavioral biometrics (such as voice or gait) with greater precision. In the case of facial recognition, AI can assess factors like depth, lighting conditions, and micro-expressions, making it harder for someone to fool the system with photos, videos, or masks. This multi-dimensional approach increases the accuracy of identification and verification processes.

For example, AI can enhance fingerprint authentication by matching the pattern of ridges and analyzing the pressure applied during the scan, the temperature of the skin, and even the moisture level. These additional data points make it significantly more difficult for an attacker to bypass the system using a replica of someone's fingerprint. Similarly, AI in voice recognition systems can detect not just the sound of a person's voice but also their speech patterns, intonation, and emotional state, ensuring a more reliable authentication process.

AI also allows for the analysis of biometric data in real time. With traditional systems, data might need to be processed after an event has occurred, which can lead to delays in identifying fraud or security breaches. However, AI-driven systems can immediately detect anomalies in the data, such as an unusual access attempt or a deviation in a user's normal behavior, and take action accordingly. This allows for proactive security measures, preventing potential threats before they cause harm.

AI's Role in Reducing Fraud and Enhancing Security

As cybercriminals become more sophisticated, the need for advanced security measures grows. One of the primary benefits of AI-driven biometric systems is their ability to reduce fraud. AI can detect patterns of fraudulent activity that might be invisible to the naked eye or traditional security systems. For instance, in financial institutions, AI can analyze large datasets of biometric information, such as fingerprints or voice recognition, to identify anomalies that could indicate identity theft or account fraud.

In a banking scenario, a customer might attempt to access their account using voice authentication. An AI system would not only recognize the voice but also cross-reference it with the person's historical interactions, analyzing speech cadence, tone, and context. If the system detects an abnormality, such as the user being unusually stressed or speaking in a different tone, it could flag the transaction for further review or require additional authentication, effectively reducing the risk of fraud.

Moreover, AI-driven biometric systems are particularly effective at combating spoofing attacks, where hackers attempt to deceive biometric systems with false inputs. For example, in facial recognition systems, AI algorithms can detect whether a presented face is natural or an image by analyzing tiny movements such as eye blinking or changes in pupil dilation. Similarly, in voice recognition, AI can distinguish between a live voice and a pre-recorded audio clip by analyzing background noise and speech characteristics. These enhanced capabilities make AI-driven biometrics far more secure than traditional systems, which are often vulnerable to simple spoofing techniques.

Continuous Learning and Adaptation

One of the most revolutionary aspects of AI-driven biometric systems is their ability to learn and adapt over time. Traditional biometric systems are often static, relying on a fixed set of data to authenticate users. However, AI systems continuously learn from new data, allowing them to evolve and improve. For example, as a person's appearance changes due to aging, weight fluctuations, or facial hair, an AI system can adjust its recognition algorithms to account for these changes. This ensures that the system remains accurate even as the user's biometric data evolves.

AI's ability to learn also extends to its capacity for pattern recognition and behavioral analysis. A typical AI-driven biometric system might start by recognizing a user based on physical characteristics such as a fingerprint or face. Over time, it can begin to incorporate behavioral data, such as the way a person types on a keyboard, the speed of their mouse movements, or even how they hold their phone. This layered approach to authentication creates a more robust security framework, making it harder for attackers to mimic both the physical and behavioral characteristics of a user.

This continuous learning capability also helps the system become more efficient in distinguishing between genuine users and impostors. For example, AI can detect subtle differences in a user's gait (the way they walk) or how they interact with a device, making it difficult for an attacker to replicate these behaviors. The more data the AI system processes, the more intelligent and precise it becomes, making it an invaluable tool in the fight against cybercrime.

Privacy Concerns and Ethical Considerations

While AI-driven biometric systems offer significant security benefits, they also raise important questions about privacy and ethics. One of the primary concerns is the collection and storage of biometric data. Since biometric information is unique and permanent, any breach of this data could have long-lasting consequences. Unlike passwords, which can be reset if compromised, biometric data such as fingerprints or facial features cannot be changed. Therefore, if hackers gain access to a database containing biometric information, the affected individuals may be at risk of identity theft or other forms of fraud for the rest of their lives.

To address these concerns, many AI-driven biometric systems are incorporating privacy-enhancing technologies such as homomorphic encryption. This advanced encryption technique allows data to be processed while still encrypted, meaning that even if the data is intercepted during processing, it remains unusable to the attacker. This ensures that biometric information is never exposed in its raw form, offering an additional layer of protection.

There is also the issue of consent and transparency. Many users may not fully understand how their biometric data is being used or shared. For example, when a person unlocks their smartphone with their fingerprint or uses facial recognition to board a flight, they might not be aware of whether that data is being stored, shared with third parties, or used for purposes beyond authentication. This lack of transparency can lead to concerns about surveillance and the potential misuse of biometric data by corporations or governments.

AI-driven biometric systems must also confront the challenge of bias. Research has shown that some biometric systems, particularly facial recognition, can have lower accuracy rates for specific demographics, such as people of color or women. This bias can result in false positives or negatives, leading to discrimination or wrongful identification. AI developers must ensure that their systems are trained on diverse datasets that reflect the variety of human appearances and behaviors to avoid these biases.

Future Trends: Quantum Computing and AI-Driven Biometric Security

Looking to the future, the combination of quantum computing and AI is expected to enhance biometric security further. Quantum computing has the potential to process vast amounts of data far more efficiently than classical computers, which could lead to faster and more secure biometric authentication methods. For example, quantum algorithms could be used to encrypt biometric data in ways that are virtually uncrackable, providing an additional layer of protection against cyberattacks.

Additionally, quantum computing could enable more sophisticated AI algorithms capable of detecting even the most subtle patterns in biometric data. This would make it even harder for attackers to bypass biometric systems using spoofing techniques or other forms of deception. As these technologies continue to evolve, AI-driven biometric systems will become even more secure and reliable, offering new possibilities for protecting privacy in the digital age.

PART 3: PRIVACY, ETHICS, AND SECURITY IN THE QUANTUM ERA

CORPORATE SURVEILLANCE AND THE BUSINESS OF DATA

In today's digital world, the way corporations collect, track, and monetize our data has fundamentally changed how businesses operate. The data we generate from online shopping habits to social media posts and web searches is valuable to companies looking to understand and influence consumer behavior. However, this comes with significant privacy concerns.

How Corporations Collect, Track, and Monetize Data

In today's hyperconnected world, the business of data is more lucrative than ever. Corporations, both large and small, are leveraging vast quantities of data to better understand their customers, refine their marketing strategies, and increase profits. The way companies collect, track, and monetize our data has become a key driver of modern business models, but it also raises significant privacy concerns for individuals.

Data Collection Methods

Corporations collect data through various channels, often without users fully realizing the extent of what is being captured. Every interaction with digital platforms, mobile apps, social media, and even physical locations can generate data that businesses can collect, store, and analyze.

- **Cookies and Web Trackers**

One of the most prevalent ways corporations collect data is by using cookies and web trackers. Cookies are small files stored on a user's device by websites they visit. While cookies can improve user experiences by remembering login details or shopping cart contents, they are also powerful tools for tracking behavior across multiple websites. Companies use cookies to build detailed profiles of users, tracking what pages they visit, how long they stay, and what links they click.

These profiles allow companies to monitor user activity not just on their site but across the web. For example, a user may search for a product on one website and see advertisements for that product on entirely different websites later. Cookies enable advertisers to track user behavior and display personalized ads based on their previous online actions.

Additionally, third-party cookies, which are placed by advertising networks, track users across multiple sites to build a detailed picture of their interests. This practice is one of the foundations of targeted advertising, which we'll explore more in the monetization section.

- **Mobile Apps and In-App Data Collection**

Mobile applications collect even more detailed information than websites, often including data on location, contacts, browsing habits within the app, and even device information. Many mobile apps, including those from reputable companies, require access to a range of personal data as part of their functionality. For example, navigation apps need access to location data, and social media apps may request access to contacts, photos, and messages.

The data collected by apps often goes beyond what is necessary for the app to function, raising concerns about privacy and user awareness. This data is invaluable to companies as it allows them to refine their products and better target their advertising efforts.

Mobile apps may also continue collecting data in the background, even when they are not actively being used. This continuous tracking can provide companies with real-time insights into user behavior, location, and preferences, all of which are valuable for creating targeted advertisements.

- **Social Media Platforms and Behavioral Data**

Social media platforms like Facebook, Instagram, and Twitter are significant players in the data collection game. These platforms are designed to encourage users to share personal information, such as their likes, dislikes, relationships, and day-to-day activities. Social media platforms collect data not only from the content users post but also from their interactions with other users' content and what they like, share, or comment on.

Social media algorithms also track the time users spend on posts, the order in which they view content, and how they interact with advertisements. By analyzing this behavioral data, platforms can build incredibly detailed profiles of their users, including interests, political beliefs, and even emotional states.

For example, Facebook uses this data to categorize users into thousands of categories that advertisers can use to target their ads. Advertisers can specify which demographics, interests, or behaviors they want to target, and Facebook will show their ads only to users who meet those criteria. This level of personalization makes social media advertising highly effective and profitable.

- **Location Tracking**

Location data is another critical piece of information that companies collect, mainly through mobile devices. Many apps track users' locations in real-time, often using GPS, Wi-Fi, or Bluetooth signals. This location data can be precious for advertisers who want to target consumers based on where they are at any given moment.

For example, a retail store may send a user a coupon when they are near one of its locations, or a restaurant might advertise lunch specials to people in the immediate area. Location tracking allows companies to provide highly personalized services, but it also means that users are constantly being monitored as they move through the physical world.

In some cases, location data is collected even when users think they have turned off tracking. Apps may access location information through alternative methods, such as Wi-Fi networks or cell towers, even when GPS tracking is disabled.

- **Purchase and Browsing History**

Online retailers and e-commerce platforms track every aspect of users' shopping habits, from what they search for to what they add to their shopping cart and ultimately purchase. Retailers like Amazon collect detailed data on their customer's shopping behavior, including the time they spend browsing certain products, the frequency with which they return to product pages, and even what products they compare before making a purchase.

This data allows companies to recommend products that are likely to appeal to users based on their previous shopping behavior. For example, after purchasing a book on Amazon, a user might receive recommendations for similar books or products that other customers bought along with that book. This personalization improves the shopping experience but also encourages users to spend more.

Retailers often share this purchase and browsing history with third parties, such as data brokers, who compile the information into detailed profiles. These profiles are then sold to advertisers or other companies looking to target specific types of consumers.

Surveillance Technologies and Biometrics

As discussed in the "Biometric Security" sections from your uploaded files, corporations are also increasingly adopting biometric technologies to track users. Biometric data includes fingerprints, facial recognition, and voice prints, which can be used for everything from unlocking a smartphone to verifying a user's identity at an airport or bank.

While biometric data provides an additional layer of security, it also raises significant privacy concerns. Once biometric data is collected, it can be difficult to protect or revoke, as it is inherently tied to an individual's identity. Companies that collect and store biometric data must ensure that this sensitive information is protected from breaches or unauthorized access.

Biometric data is precious to corporations because it provides a unique and irrefutable identifier for everyone. This makes it easier for companies to track users across multiple platforms and services, further enhancing their ability to build detailed consumer profiles.

Data Tracking Techniques

After collecting data, corporations use various tracking techniques to follow users across platforms, devices, and even offline activities. The goal of tracking is to gather as much information as possible about a user's behavior, preferences, and habits.

- **Cross-Device Tracking**

In today's digital landscape, people use multiple devices to access the internet, such as smartphones, tablets, laptops, and smart TVs. Corporations employ cross-device tracking techniques to monitor users across all these devices. This allows them to build a comprehensive picture of a user's online behavior, regardless of whether they are browsing on their phone or making a purchase on their computer.

Cross-device tracking uses a combination of cookies, device identifiers, and algorithms to link activity across different devices. For example, a user might search for a product on their phone and later purchase it on their laptop. Cross-device tracking enables the advertiser to recognize that these actions were taken by the same person, even though they occurred on different devices.

- **Social Plugins and Widgets**

Many websites incorporate social plugins and widgets, such as Facebook "Like" buttons or Twitter "Share" buttons. These plugins allow users to interact with social media platforms directly from other websites. However, they also allow social media companies to track users' behavior on those external websites, even if the user doesn't click on the plugin.

For example, suppose a user visits a news website with a Facebook "Like" button. In that case, Facebook can track that user's visit and add that information to the user's profile, even if the user doesn't interact with the button. This gives social media platforms an additional method of tracking users beyond their websites and apps.

- **Third-Party Data Sharing and Data Brokers**

Corporations often share the data they collect with third parties, such as data brokers. Data brokers compile information from multiple sources, such as websites, apps, social media, public records, and more, to create comprehensive consumer profiles. These profiles may include everything from demographic information to purchase history, browsing behavior, and even health and financial data.

Data brokers then sell these profiles to other companies, including advertisers, insurance companies, and financial institutions. For example, an insurance company might use data from a broker to determine whether someone is likely to file a claim, or an advertiser might use the data to target specific demographics with ads for luxury products.

Third-party data sharing is particularly problematic from a privacy perspective because users often have no control over how their data is shared or sold. Even if a user takes steps to limit data collection on one platform, their information may still be shared or sold by other companies without their knowledge or consent.

How Corporations Monetize Data

Data is not just a resource; it has become a significant driver of revenue for corporations. By analyzing and selling data, companies can significantly boost their profits. The most common ways corporations monetize data include targeted advertising, selling data to third parties, and using data for predictive analytics.

- **Targeted Advertising**

Targeted advertising is one primary way corporations monetize the data they collect. Advertisers pay a premium to show personalized ads to individuals based on their behavior, interests, and demographics.

For instance, Google and Facebook allow advertisers to target specific users based on the data collected from their searches, clicks, likes, and shares. This means that an advertiser can choose to show ads only to people who are interested in fitness, have recently searched for workout gear, and live in a particular region. This level of personalization increases the effectiveness of ads, making them more valuable to advertisers and more profitable for platforms.

- **Data as a Product**

Some companies go a step further and sell their data directly as a product. Data brokers purchase data from various sources and sell it to companies looking to gain insights into their customers. The value of this data lies in the detailed consumer profiles it creates, which can be used to predict behavior, tailor products, and optimize marketing strategies.

In other cases, companies use their data to create new services, such as predictive analytics platforms or customer relationship management (CRM) systems, which help other businesses make data-driven decisions.

How Corporations Monetize Data

In today's digital economy, personal data has become one of the most valuable commodities. Every action taken online, whether browsing a website, making a purchase, or interacting on social media, generates data that corporations eagerly collect. This data is transformed into actionable insights, which are then used to influence consumer behavior, optimize business operations, and generate significant revenue streams. But how exactly do corporations monetize this data, and what does that mean for the average user?

1. Targeted Advertising: Precision Marketing at Scale

One of the primary ways corporations monetize data is through targeted advertising. Unlike traditional forms of advertising, where companies would pay for broad campaigns aimed at large audiences, targeted advertising allows businesses to deliver highly personalized ads based on specific user profiles. These profiles are built using vast amounts of data collected from various sources, including:

- **Browsing habits**: Corporations track which websites you visit, how long you stay on each page, and what content you interact with. This information helps them understand your interests and preferences.

- **Purchase history**: If you've ever bought a product online, that information is stored and used to suggest similar products or services in the future.

- **Demographic data**: Age, gender, location, and income level are often inferred or directly collected from users, allowing for precise targeting.

For instance, if a user searches for hiking gear on an e-commerce site, that information can be shared or sold to advertisers, who then display ads for outdoor equipment across different platforms. This form of precision marketing maximizes the effectiveness of advertising campaigns by targeting users who are most likely to be interested in the product, increasing the likelihood of a purchase.

From the perspective of advertisers, this practice is invaluable. By focusing their efforts on users who are already inclined to engage with their products, they can significantly boost conversion rates and reduce wasted advertising spend. Companies like Google and Facebook have built entire business models around this, earning billions of dollars annually from targeted advertising.

2. Selling Data to Third Parties: The Data Brokerage Economy

While many corporations use data to improve their operations, a significant portion of this data is also sold to third-party data brokers. These brokers compile data from multiple sources, creating comprehensive profiles of individuals that go far beyond what any single company could achieve on its own. These profiles often include detailed information on:

- **Consumer behavior**: What products people buy, how often they shop, and how much they spend.

- **Lifestyle information**: Data on hobbies, interests, and even political or religious views.

- **Personal characteristics**: Age, marital status, income level, and occupation.

Data brokers then sell this information to companies in various industries, from retail and finance to insurance and healthcare. For example, an insurance company might purchase data to assess the risk profile of potential customers and adjust premium rates accordingly. Similarly, a retailer might buy data to understand consumer trends better and tailor its marketing strategies.

One of the most concerning aspects of this practice is the lack of transparency. In many cases, users are unaware that their data is being sold, and they have little control over how it is used. While companies may include clauses about data sharing in their privacy policies, these documents are often written in complex legal language, making it difficult for users to understand the implications fully.

3. Predictive Analytics: Anticipating Future Behavior

Another powerful tool in data monetization is predictive analytics. By analyzing historical data, companies can make informed predictions about future behavior, allowing them to anticipate consumer needs and act accordingly. This capability is precious in industries like retail, finance, and healthcare, where being able to predict trends or behaviors can lead to significant competitive advantages.

For example, an e-commerce platform might analyze a user's purchase history to predict what products they are likely to buy next. If a user frequently buys baby products, the platform might infer that they are a new parent and recommend related items like toys, diapers, or baby clothes. This proactive approach not only increases the likelihood of a sale but also enhances customer satisfaction by making the shopping experience more convenient and personalized.

In the financial sector, predictive analytics can identify potential loan applicants who are more likely to default, allowing lenders to adjust their terms or reject high-risk individuals. Similarly, in healthcare, predictive models can anticipate patient needs, enabling providers to offer more timely and personalized care.

While predictive analytics offers substantial benefits for businesses, it also raises significant privacy concerns. Users may not be comfortable with companies making assumptions about their behavior, primarily when those assumptions are based on deeply personal data.

4. Personalized Services: Enhancing User Experience for Profit

Many companies use the data they collect to offer personalized services that enhance the user experience. This is particularly common in the entertainment, retail, and technology industries. For instance:

- **Streaming services** like Netflix and Spotify use algorithms to analyze users' viewing or listening habits, recommending new content that aligns with their preferences. This not only keeps users engaged but also increases the time they spend on the platform, ultimately generating more revenue for the company.

- **E-commerce platforms** like Amazon use purchase history and browsing behavior to recommend products that users are likely to be interested in, making it easier for them to find what they need and encouraging additional purchases.

While these personalized services can improve the user experience, they also serve as powerful tools for increasing customer retention and driving sales. The more personalized a service becomes, the more likely users are to continue using it, which means more data for the company and more opportunities to monetize that data.

5. Data as a Product: The Rise of Data-Driven Business Models

In some cases, corporations have developed entirely new business models centered around selling access to their data. For example, companies like Facebook and Google allow advertisers to access their vast troves of user data to create highly targeted advertising campaigns. This data-as-a-product approach has become a cornerstone of the digital advertising industry, enabling companies to generate substantial revenue without directly selling goods or services.

Google's search engine, for instance, operates on this principle. While the service is free for users, Google makes billions by selling advertising space that leverages user search data. Advertisers bid for the opportunity to display ads to users based on their search queries, interests, and browsing habits, making the platform highly profitable.

Similarly, social media platforms like Facebook generate revenue by offering advertisers the ability to target users based on their detailed demographic and behavioral data. These platforms collect vast amounts of information about users' interactions, preferences, and social networks, which they then use to help advertisers create more effective ad campaigns.

6. Loyalty Programs and Rewards: Collecting Data through Incentives

Loyalty programs are another way corporations collect and monetize data. By offering rewards or discounts, companies encourage customers to sign up for programs that track their spending habits, purchase preferences, and even location data. In exchange for points or discounts, users willingly provide detailed information that the company can use to improve its marketing strategies and product offerings.

For example, grocery stores often offer loyalty cards that give customers access to special deals. In return, the store collects data on every purchase the customer makes, allowing them to build a detailed profile of the individual's shopping habits. This data is then used to tailor marketing efforts, such as sending personalized coupons or suggesting related products.

Loyalty programs also allow companies to track customer retention and identify patterns that can help them improve customer satisfaction and increase revenue. By understanding why customers stay loyal and why they leave, businesses can refine their strategies and enhance their services.

Actionable Solutions to Mitigate Corporate Surveillance Risks

As digital users, we leave a wealth of personal information scattered across the web, often without realizing the extent to which corporations collect, track, and monetize this data. However, mitigating the risks posed by corporate surveillance is possible with a series of proactive steps. These solutions, drawn from real-world examples, aim to empower individuals to regain control over their digital footprints. By understanding how data is collected and implementing privacy-conscious practices, we can reduce exposure to corporate surveillance.

1. Privacy-Focused Browsers and Search Engines

Most mainstream browsers and search engines, such as Google and Chrome, rely heavily on tracking user behavior to deliver personalized ads and content. However, some alternatives prioritize user privacy by not collecting or sharing user data.

- **Privacy-Focused Browsers**: Browsers like **Brave and Mozilla Firefox** offer built-in privacy tools that block ads, trackers, and third-party cookies by default. Brave, for example, blocks cross-site trackers that would otherwise follow your activity across different websites. It also features an integrated ad blocker, providing an extra layer of privacy from advertising companies that thrive on user data.

- **Search Engines that Don't Track**: DuckDuckGo and Start Page are two search engines designed with privacy in mind. DuckDuckGo does not track your searches or store your personal information, making it an excellent alternative to Google, which collects vast amounts of data about your search queries, location, and behavior.

By switching to these tools, users can significantly reduce the data collected on them while still enjoying the convenience of browsing the web.

2. Regularly Clear Cookies and Browsing History

Cookies, while often helpful in remembering login information or personalizing websites, also pose a significant privacy risk. Many companies use third-party cookies to track your browsing activity across multiple sites, creating a detailed profile of your interests and behavior.

- **Managing Cookies**: Regularly clearing your cookies can prevent companies from building long-term profiles based on your browsing habits. Most browsers, such as Chrome, Firefox, and Safari, allow users to automatically delete cookies after each session or block third-party cookies entirely.

- **Private Browsing or Incognito Mode**: Browsers also offer features like "private browsing" or "incognito mode," which prevent the storage of browsing history, cookies, and form data. While this doesn't stop websites from tracking your activity while you're online, it does ensure that once the session is closed, no data remains on your device.

Additionally, some browser extensions, like Privacy Badger or uBlock Origin, block third-party cookies and tracking scripts automatically. By using these tools, users can further protect themselves from being tracked across the web.

3. Enable Do Not Track Features

Most modern browsers have a "Do Not Track" (DNT) feature. When enabled, this setting asks websites not to track your browsing activity. While not all websites honor this request, it's still worth enabling as it signals your preference to limit tracking.

- **How DNT Works**: By enabling this feature, you inform websites that you do not want to be tracked for purposes such as targeted advertising. Although compliance is voluntary, some sites and companies respect this request. Additionally, in regions with stronger privacy laws, such as the European Union under the General Data Protection Regulation (GDPR), websites may be more likely to honor DNT settings.

To enable DNT:

- **Chrome**: Settings > Privacy and Security > Send a "Do Not Track" request with your browsing traffic.

- **Firefox**: Settings > Privacy and Security > Enable "Send websites a 'Do Not Track' signal."

- **Safari**: Preferences > Privacy > Prevent cross-site tracking.

4. Limit Data Sharing on Social Media Platforms

Social media platforms like Facebook, Twitter, and Instagram are among the most significant collectors of personal data. They gather information about what you share, who you interact with, where you log in from, and even track your browsing behavior outside their platforms.

- **Review and Update Privacy Settings**: Each platform has privacy settings that allow users to control how much data is shared with third parties. On Facebook, for example, users can adjust their settings to limit who can see their posts, personal information, and friend lists. You can also turn off Facebook's ad preferences to prevent it from using your activity across other websites to target ads.

- **Limit App Permissions**: Many social media platforms allow third-party apps to access your data. It's essential to review the permissions you've granted and revoke access to any apps you no longer use or trust. For example, on Facebook, navigate to "Apps and Websites" under settings and remove any third-party apps that no longer need access to your information.

- **Disable Location Sharing**: Social media apps often request access to your location, even when it's not necessary for the app's functionality. To protect your privacy, consider disabling location services for apps like Instagram and Facebook unless you need them for specific purposes (e.g., location tagging in photos).

5. Use Virtual Private Networks (VPNs)

A **Virtual Private Network (VPN)** is one of the most effective tools for maintaining privacy online. A VPN works by encrypting your internet traffic and routing it through a server in a different location, masking your

IP address and making it difficult for companies or hackers to track your online activities.

- **How VPNs Protect Your Data**: VPNs make it more difficult for websites and advertisers to link your browsing activity to your real identity. This is especially useful when using public Wi-Fi networks, which are often vulnerable to surveillance and hacking attempts. With a VPN, your data is encrypted, meaning that even if someone intercepts your traffic, they won't be able to read it.

- **Choosing a Privacy-Respecting VPN**: Not all VPNs are created equal. Some VPNs may keep logs of your browsing activity, defeating the purpose of using a VPN in the first place. It's crucial to choose a VPN service that has a strict no-logs policy, such as **ExpressVPN**, **NordVPN**, or **ProtonVPN**.

6. Be Mindful of Permissions When Using Apps

Many apps request more permissions than they need to function, such as access to your contacts, camera, or location data. For instance, a photo-editing app might ask for access to your location, even though location data isn't necessary for its core functionality. This kind of unnecessary data collection poses a significant privacy risk.

- **Review App Permissions**: Go into your phone settings and review the permissions each app has been granted. On both iOS and Android, you can limit which apps have access to sensitive data like your location, contacts, or microphone. Regularly audit these permissions and revoke access when it's not necessary.

- **Use Permission Prompts Wisely**: When installing new apps, be cautious about granting permissions. If an app requests access to information it doesn't need, deny the request. You can always grant permissions later if necessary.

7. Opt-Out of Data Collection Programs

Many companies provide users with the option to opt out of data collection or personalized advertising programs. For instance, Google and Facebook allow users to turn off interest-based ads, which means they won't use your browsing history or profile information to show you targeted ads.

- **Google's Data Privacy Settings**: Google offers users the ability to adjust their ad preferences and control what data is collected. By visiting the **Google Ad Settings** page, you can turn off ad personalization, which stops Google from using your search history and other personal data to serve targeted ads.

- **Data Brokers and Opting Out**: Data broker companies that collect and sell personal data often have opt-out mechanisms on their websites. You can use tools like Delete Me to remove your personal information from databases that data brokers sell to third parties. Additionally, some browsers now include "Global Privacy Control" features that help you opt out of tracking.

8. Use Encrypted Communication Tools

Messaging apps like Signal, WhatsApp, and Telegram offer end-to-end encryption, which means that your messages can only be read by you and the intended recipient. This level of encryption ensures that your communications remain private and can't be intercepted by third parties, including corporations that might otherwise analyze your conversations for targeted advertising.

- **Signal**: Known for its privacy-first approach, Signal offers strong end-to-end encryption for messaging and voice/video calls. Unlike other messaging apps, Signal does not collect user data, making it a top choice for privacy-conscious individuals.

- **WhatsApp**: While WhatsApp also provides end-to-end encryption, it's owned by Facebook, which has a history of data collection. While your messages are encrypted, Facebook still collects metadata, such as who you communicate with and how often. For the highest level of privacy, Signal remains the preferred option.

Quantum Computing's Impact on Data Monetization

Quantum computing is poised to revolutionize various industries, and data monetization is no exception. As businesses increasingly rely on data to drive profits, the enhanced computational power of quantum computers opens new possibilities for how data can be collected, processed, analyzed, and ultimately monetized. While traditional computing has already enabled corporations to gather and exploit massive amounts of data, quantum computing will push the boundaries of what's possible in terms of speed, complexity, and depth of analysis.

What is Quantum Computing, and How Does it Differ?

To understand its impact on data monetization, it's essential to grasp how quantum computing works first. Traditional computers operate using bits, which are binary units that represent either a 0 or a 1. This binary system limits the operations to sequential tasks. On the other hand, quantum computers use *qubits*, which can exist in multiple states simultaneously, thanks to the principles of superposition and entanglement. This allows quantum computers to process vast amounts of data at once, handling multiple computations simultaneously and solving complex problems far faster than any classical computer could.

For businesses, the introduction of quantum computing will mean exponentially faster processing times and the ability to analyze larger datasets with greater accuracy. This kind of computational power opens new avenues for data monetization, with far-reaching consequences for industries that rely on big data.

One of the most immediate benefits of quantum computing is its ability to process data much faster than traditional computers. In the current digital landscape, companies collect vast amounts of data from users, ranging from their browsing habits and social media interactions to their online shopping behavior. Analyzing this data can be time-consuming and computationally intensive, especially when working with massive datasets.

With quantum computing, these challenges are minimized. Businesses will be able to process petabytes of data in a fraction of the time it would take traditional systems, allowing for real-time analysis and faster decision-making. This not only increases efficiency but also provides companies with a competitive advantage, enabling them to act on data-driven insights more quickly than ever before. For instance, personalized advertising campaigns could be developed and deployed almost instantaneously based on real-time consumer behavior, thereby increasing the effectiveness of targeted marketing strategies.

Moreover, quantum computers will enhance the ability to analyze complex datasets that involve multiple variables and dynamic interactions, such as weather patterns, financial markets, or consumer behavior. This will enable businesses to make more accurate predictions, optimize pricing strategies, and develop highly targeted marketing campaigns, all of which are key to data monetization.

As data becomes more integral to decision-making across industries, the ability to make accurate predictions about future trends is invaluable. Current predictive analytics relies heavily on machine learning models that sift through large datasets to find patterns and make forecasts. However, these models are limited by the computational power of classical computers, which struggle with the complexity and scale of the datasets being analyzed.

Quantum computing changes this paradigm by providing the processing power necessary to handle even the most complex datasets. For instance, while a classical computer may analyze past consumer behavior to predict future purchases, a quantum computer can simultaneously evaluate multiple variables, such as time, location, and socio-economic factors, to make far more accurate predictions.

With quantum computing, businesses will be able to develop hyper-personalized marketing strategies. These strategies will allow businesses to predict not only what consumers will buy but also when, where, and how they are likely to make their purchases. This level of insight can drive substantial increases in conversion rates and customer loyalty, leading to higher revenues and better customer satisfaction.

For instance, e-commerce companies will be able to predict when a consumer is likely to run out of a product they purchased earlier and target them with timely ads or promotions. Similarly, financial institutions can use quantum-powered predictive models to assess risk more accurately and make better investment decisions. The possibilities are virtually endless, as quantum computing enables businesses to turn vast amounts of raw data into actionable insights faster and more accurately than ever before.

Quantum Encryption and Data Security: A Double-Edged Sword

While quantum computing offers exciting possibilities for data monetization, it also poses significant challenges, particularly in data security. Quantum computers can break the encryption methods currently used to secure sensitive data. Encryption methods like RSA and ECC (Elliptic Curve Cryptography), which rely on the difficulty of factoring large numbers, are vulnerable to quantum attacks. A powerful quantum computer could break these encryption keys in mere seconds, exposing sensitive data that was previously thought to be secure.

This creates a paradox for businesses. On one hand, quantum computing will enable companies to process and monetize data faster and more efficiently. On the other hand, it also creates new vulnerabilities in data security, potentially undermining consumer trust and leading to significant legal and financial liabilities.

To address this challenge, businesses will need to adopt quantum-safe encryption algorithms that can withstand the computational power of quantum computers. One such approach is quantum key distribution (QKD), which uses the principles of quantum mechanics to distribute encryption keys securely. In QKD, any attempt to intercept the encryption key would disturb the quantum system and alert the parties involved, ensuring the security of the data.

As companies develop quantum-resistant encryption techniques, they will also need to invest in infrastructure that can support these advanced security measures. This could include upgrading their data centers, securing cloud storage solutions, and implementing more stringent data governance policies. The ability to securely store and transmit data in the quantum era will become a key differentiator for businesses, especially those that handle large amounts of sensitive information, such as financial institutions, healthcare providers, and government agencies.

Revolutionizing Business Models and Data Services

Quantum computing will not only accelerate existing data monetization practices but also give rise to entirely new business models. Companies that previously focused on collecting and analyzing data may transition to offering **quantum-powered analytics services** as a standalone product. For example, cloud service providers like Amazon Web Services (AWS) and Google Cloud are already exploring the potential of quantum computing, and, likely, they will soon offer quantum-powered data analysis tools as part of their services.

Smaller businesses that lack the resources to develop their quantum computing capabilities will be able to purchase access to these services on a subscription basis. This will allow them to leverage the power of quantum analytics without the need for substantial infrastructure investments. This could democratize access to advanced data processing capabilities, enabling companies of all sizes to benefit from quantum computing.

Additionally, industries such as healthcare, finance, and retail, which rely heavily on data analysis, will be able to utilize quantum computing to create more personalized products and services. In healthcare, for example, quantum computers could analyze genetic data and patient histories to provide tailored treatment plans that improve patient outcomes. Similarly, financial institutions could use quantum-powered risk models to develop personalized investment portfolios for their clients, considering a wider range of factors than is currently possible.

Quantum Computing and the Future of Data Privacy

As quantum computing becomes more widespread, concerns about data privacy will emerge. The ability to process vast amounts of data in real time could lead to unprecedented levels of surveillance and data tracking. Governments and corporations could use quantum computers to sift through enormous datasets and uncover patterns that were previously undetectable, raising ethical questions about privacy and consent.

For instance, the use of quantum computing in conjunction with facial recognition technology could allow for real-time surveillance of entire populations. While this might be justified in terms of national security or crime prevention, it also represents a significant invasion of privacy. As quantum computing enables more comprehensive data collection and analysis, regulators will need to step in to ensure that the rights of individuals are protected.

Furthermore, the threat of quantum-enabled cyberattacks could erode consumer trust in how businesses handle their data. As companies begin to adopt quantum computing technologies, they will need to be transparent about how they collect, store, and use data. In this sense, **data ethics** will become a critical component of corporate governance, and businesses that prioritize data privacy and transparency will have a competitive advantage in the quantum era.

GOVERNMENT SURVEILLANCE: BALANCING PRIVACY AND NATIONAL SECURITY

Mass Surveillance Programs and Their Global Implications

Mass surveillance refers to the large-scale monitoring of individuals' activities by governments or other entities, typically carried out in the name of national security, law enforcement, or public safety. The advent of advanced technology, such as the internet, mobile devices, and cloud computing, has made it easier for governments worldwide to collect vast amounts of data about their citizens. While these programs are often justified as necessary for protecting the public from crime, terrorism, and cyber threats, they raise significant concerns about personal privacy, civil liberties, and the potential for abuse.

Major Global Mass Surveillance Programs

Various governments around the world have implemented sophisticated surveillance programs that tap into communication networks, social media, and personal devices. Let's explore some of the most notable examples:

1. **PRISM (United States):** PRISM is a clandestine mass electronic surveillance data-mining program launched by the U.S. National Security Agency (NSA) in 2007. It was publicly revealed by former NSA contractor Edward Snowden in 2013. The PRISM program allows the NSA to collect and analyze internet communications from major U.S. tech companies like Google, Facebook, Microsoft, and

Apple. PRISM collects metadata, emails, chat messages, video calls, and other forms of digital communication from both U.S. citizens and foreign nationals, purportedly in the name of national security.

The global implications of PRISM are far-reaching. As the U.S. controls many major internet platforms and services used worldwide, PRISM extends its surveillance beyond American borders, affecting users globally. Many foreign governments criticized the program, claiming it violated international privacy laws and undermined trust between the U.S. and its allies. Critics argue that PRISM, while aimed at stopping terrorism, poses a threat to privacy and freedom of expression.

2. **Tempora (United Kingdom):** The Tempora program, operated by the Government Communications Headquarters (GCHQ) in the United Kingdom, is another mass surveillance initiative. Tempora taps into fiber-optic cables to intercept internet and phone traffic on a massive scale. The data is stored for analysis, and the program collects both content (e.g., emails and social media messages) and metadata (e.g., phone call records and IP addresses). Tempora collaborates closely with the NSA and other intelligence agencies, sharing data and insights.

The global implications of Tempora are significant because much of the world's internet traffic passes through UK-based servers. This gives GCHQ unprecedented access to international communications. Like PRISM, Tempora has been criticized for its broad scope and lack of transparency. Concerns have been raised about the potential for misuse, especially since much of the data is collected without explicit consent from individuals or companies.

3. **China's Social Credit System:** China's Social Credit System is perhaps the most extensive and controversial example of mass surveillance in the modern world. This system tracks the behaviors, actions, and communications of Chinese citizens and assigns them a social credit score. The score reflects how well an individual adheres to the government's expectations in areas such as financial responsibility, legal compliance, and even social behavior. A low social credit score can lead to penalties such as travel restrictions, denial of loans, or exclusion from specific jobs.

China's surveillance infrastructure includes extensive use of facial recognition technology, AI-driven monitoring, and an expansive network of cameras that track citizens' movements in public spaces. The social credit system has raised alarm bells among human rights advocates, who argue that it represents an unprecedented level of government control over citizens' lives. Furthermore, China's surveillance technology has been exported to other countries, leading to concerns about the spread of authoritarian surveillance practices worldwide.

4. **Russia's SORM (System for Operative Investigative Activities):** Russia's SORM program is a comprehensive surveillance system that allows the government to intercept internet communications, mobile phone traffic, and emails. All internet service providers (ISPs) and telecommunications companies operating in Russia are required to install special equipment that provides the Federal Security Service (FSB) direct access to user data. SORM has been used to monitor activists, opposition figures, and ordinary citizens.

Globally, SORM has drawn attention for its role in limiting free speech and cracking down on dissent. Russia's surveillance practices highlight how mass surveillance programs can be used not only for national security but also for political control. The international community has voiced concerns about the erosion of privacy and civil liberties in Russia, particularly as the government expands its digital monitoring capabilities.

5. **India's Aadhaar:** India's Aadhaar program is the world's most extensive biometric identification system, with over a billion citizens enrolled. The system collects fingerprints, iris scans, and demographic data to create a unique identification number for each citizen. While initially designed to streamline welfare distribution and reduce fraud, Aadhaar has expanded into a tool for mass surveillance. The system is now used for everything from banking and mobile phone verification to voting and healthcare access.

The global implications of Aadhaar lie in its potential to inspire other countries to adopt similar biometric identification systems. While Aadhaar has benefits, such as improved access to government services, it has also raised concerns about privacy and data security. There have been instances of data breaches and unauthorized access to personal information, sparking debates about the balance between efficiency and individual rights.

The Privacy Trade-Off: Security vs. Freedom

The justification for mass surveillance is typically framed around national security and crime prevention. Governments argue that, in an increasingly digital world, monitoring internet traffic, phone calls, and other communications is necessary to identify and neutralize threats. In many cases, mass surveillance programs have been credited with preventing terrorist attacks, thwarting criminal activity, and securing sensitive information from foreign adversaries.

However, these benefits come at the cost of personal privacy. The more governments monitor their citizens, the less room there is for private, unobserved communication. This trade-off between security and freedom is a central ethical dilemma in the surveillance debate.

1.   **Privacy as a Fundamental Right:** Privacy is widely regarded as a fundamental human right. The United Nations Universal Declaration of Human Rights (UDHR) recognizes the right to privacy, stating that "no one shall be subjected to arbitrary interference with his privacy, family, home, or correspondence." However, in the face of mass surveillance, this right is increasingly compromised. Individuals are often unaware of the extent to which their data is being collected, analyzed, and stored.

The problem is further complicated by the fact that many mass surveillance programs operate in secrecy. Citizens may not have the ability to opt out of surveillance or understand how their data is being used. This lack of transparency undermines trust in government institutions and raises questions about accountability.

2.   **The Chilling Effect:** Another significant consequence of mass surveillance is the "chilling effect" on free speech and expression. When individuals know they are being watched, they may be less likely to express controversial opinions, participate in protests, or engage in activities that could be perceived as dissenting. This is especially concerning in authoritarian regimes, where mass surveillance is often used to stifle opposition and silence critics.

Even in democratic countries, the fear of surveillance can lead to self-censorship. People may avoid discussing sensitive topics online or refrain from visiting certain websites out of fear that government agencies could misinterpret their actions.

3.   **Data Security Risks:** The vast amounts of data collected through mass surveillance programs also pose significant security risks. While governments claim to store this data securely, history has shown that no system is entirely immune to breaches. High-profile cases such as the Edward Snowden revelations and the WikiLeaks disclosures have exposed the vulnerability of government surveillance data to leaks and hacks.

Moreover, governments' collection of personal data creates a valuable target for cybercriminals. If hackers were to gain access to surveillance databases, they could exploit personal information for identity theft, financial fraud, or blackmail. The more data governments collect, the greater the risk of a catastrophic breach.

Global Implications of Mass Surveillance

The global implications of mass surveillance extend beyond individual privacy concerns. As countries develop more sophisticated surveillance technologies, the balance of power in the international arena shifts. Nations with advanced surveillance capabilities can exert greater control over their populations and influence global politics.

1.   International Tensions

Mass surveillance programs can strain diplomatic relations between countries. For example, the revelations about PRISM created tension between the U.S. and its allies, particularly those in Europe. Many European leaders expressed outrage over the U.S. government's access to their citizens' data, leading to discussions about data sovereignty and the need for stronger privacy protections in international agreements.

2. The Export of Surveillance Technologies

Another global implication is the export of surveillance technologies to authoritarian regimes. Countries with advanced surveillance infrastructures, like China and Russia, have begun exporting their technologies to other nations, particularly in Africa and the Middle East. These technologies are often used to monitor and suppress political opposition, limiting democratic freedoms.

The spread of surveillance technologies to countries with poor human rights records raises ethical concerns. It highlights the need for international regulations governing the sale and use of surveillance tools and greater accountability for governments that abuse these systems.

3. The Role of Tech Companies

Finally, the role of tech companies in mass surveillance cannot be overlooked. Many government surveillance programs rely on data provided by private companies. In some cases, tech giants like Google, Facebook, and Apple are compelled to share user data with governments. This creates a complex dynamic where private companies are both enablers and potential protectors of privacy.

Some tech companies have taken steps to protect their users' privacy, such as implementing end-to-end encryption and refusing to comply with government requests for data. However, in countries with strict surveillance laws, tech companies may be forced to cooperate with the government or risk losing their ability to operate.

PRIVACY RIGHTS AND ETHICAL CHALLENGES

The concept of privacy has evolved dramatically in the digital age. Privacy is no longer just about protecting our personal space from physical intrusion. It now extends into the online world, where every click, transaction, and interaction leaves a digital trace. As more of our lives migrate to the digital realm, the question of how governments handle surveillance and protect privacy has taken on new dimensions.

In democratic societies, privacy is considered a fundamental human right. The right to privacy includes freedom from unwarranted intrusion, the ability to communicate without interference, and the assurance that personal data won't be misused or exploited. However, in the context of mass surveillance, governments often argue that these rights must sometimes be curtailed for the greater good, particularly in the name of national security.

This creates a significant ethical dilemma: How do we balance the need for national security with the protection of individual privacy rights? As surveillance technologies become more advanced and invasive, the ethical challenges around privacy intensify. Below are some of the significant ethical concerns that have emerged in the age of digital surveillance.

Informed Consent and Transparency: How Much Should Citizens Know?

One of the most significant ethical challenges in government surveillance is the lack of informed consent and transparency. In many instances, surveillance programs operate in secret, leaving citizens unaware that their data is being collected, analyzed, or stored by their government. The lack of transparency erodes public trust and prevents individuals from making informed decisions about their privacy.

For example, the *PRISM* program, which Edward Snowden revealed, was shrouded in secrecy. The public did not know that the U.S. government was collecting vast amounts of data from major tech companies like Google, Facebook, and Apple. This included emails, chat messages, and video calls, as well as information that most people assumed was private. The program operated without the explicit consent of the individuals being monitored, raising serious ethical questions about transparency and the right to privacy.

According to the principles of informed consent, individuals should have the right to know when, why, and how their data is being collected. In the physical world, this might mean being informed when surveillance cameras are installed in public spaces. In the digital world, however, it's more complicated. Governments often justify the lack of transparency by citing national security concerns. But does the need for secrecy justify infringing on the privacy rights of millions of people? This is where ethical tensions begin to surface.

From the perspective of privacy advocates, transparency is crucial for accountability. Without it, governments can engage in overreach, exploiting surveillance powers to suppress dissent or invade the lives of citizens without cause. This lack of oversight is one of the core ethical issues in modern surveillance. Citizens should be able to give informed consent or at least be made aware of the scope and purpose of the data collection happening around them.

Surveillance, Data Misuse, and the Risk of Abuse

Government surveillance raises serious concerns about data misuse. Once collected, how is this data used? Who has access to it? And what safeguards are in place to ensure that it isn't exploited for nefarious purposes?

One of the biggest ethical dangers of mass surveillance is the potential for abuse. Governments might collect data with the intention of protecting national security, but this data can be repurposed for political, commercial, or other non-legitimate goals. For instance, in some authoritarian regimes, surveillance is used not just to fight crime but also to monitor and control political opponents, journalists, and activists. This kind of surveillance undermines the principles of democracy and free speech.

Moreover, once data is collected, it becomes a target for cyberattacks. Hackers, both state-sponsored and independent, can exploit government databases, exposing sensitive personal information to malicious actors. High-profile data breaches have demonstrated the vulnerability of even the most secure systems. When governments collect massive amounts of data through surveillance programs, they also create a lucrative target for cybercriminals. The ethical responsibility, then, extends beyond data collection to include securing that data against misuse and breaches.

In addition, governments may be tempted to share the data they collect with other nations or sell it to private companies. In one of my books titled Unveiling Privacy, the concept of data monetization is highlighted as a significant issue in modern surveillance. Corporations already collect and sell vast amounts of user data, often without users' consent. Government surveillance programs could easily fall into this same trap, using collected data for commercial purposes, which could lead to a significant erosion of trust.

Ethically, this raises the question of ownership: Who owns the data collected by the government? Does the government have the right to share, sell, or repurpose that data without the individual's consent? The answer to these questions is not straightforward, but they underscore the need for robust data protection laws that define the limits of how surveillance data can be used.

Discrimination, Profiling, and Targeted Surveillance

Another major ethical issue in government surveillance is the risk of discrimination and profiling. Surveillance programs, particularly those powered by AI, can disproportionately target specific groups based on race, religion, political beliefs, or geographic location. This form of targeted surveillance raises serious ethical concerns about equality, fairness, and non-discrimination.

For example, after 9/11, many surveillance programs in the U.S. and other countries focused heavily on Muslim communities, often profiling individuals based solely on their religion. Similarly, surveillance programs in different nations have disproportionately targeted ethnic minorities, political dissidents, or activists. This raises the specter of

racial profiling, where specific communities are unfairly subjected to heightened scrutiny simply because of their identity.

The use of **AI** in surveillance only exacerbates this problem. AI algorithms are not neutral; they are trained on data that often reflect the biases of the societies that create them. This means that AI-driven surveillance programs can replicate and amplify existing biases. For example, AI systems used for facial recognition have been shown to be less accurate in identifying people of color, which can lead to false positives and wrongful targeting. In such cases, individuals may be flagged as suspicious or guilty based solely on flawed algorithmic assessments.

Ethically, this form of surveillance violates the principle of equality before the law. No group should be unfairly targeted or discriminated against, but in practice, surveillance systems often fail to uphold this standard. To address this, governments must ensure that surveillance programs are designed with fairness and transparency in mind and that they do not contribute to systemic bias or discrimination.

Data Security and Protection: Who Guards the Guardians?

Even when surveillance programs are implemented with the best intentions, data security remains a significant ethical challenge. How can governments ensure that the data they collect is kept secure and protected from unauthorized access?

As highlighted in my *Zero Trust* book, one of the biggest challenges facing modern cybersecurity is ensuring that sensitive data doesn't fall into the wrong hands. This is especially true for government surveillance programs, which often collect massive amounts of personal information. If this data is not adequately protected, it can become a target for hackers, foreign governments, or even rogue employees within the surveillance agencies themselves.

The ethical responsibility of protecting surveillance data falls squarely on the shoulders of the government. Failing to do so can result in catastrophic breaches that compromise the privacy and security of millions of citizens. In the worst cases, such breaches can lead to identity theft, financial fraud, or even physical harm if sensitive information about individuals' locations or activities is exposed.

To mitigate these risks, many surveillance systems are moving toward a zero-trust model, where every entity, whether inside or outside the system, is assumed to be a potential threat. This model requires continuous monitoring, encryption, and rigorous authentication protocols. However, even with these measures in place, data breaches are always a possibility. Governments must invest heavily in cybersecurity measures to ensure that surveillance data is adequately protected.

Moreover, robust oversight is needed to prevent abuse from within. Governments and intelligence agencies wield immense power through surveillance programs, and without proper checks and balances, this power can be easily misused. Ethical governance of these programs requires independent oversight bodies, transparency reports, and strict accountability measures to prevent overreach and ensure that surveillance powers are used appropriately.

The Ethical Imperative of Preserving Privacy

At its core, the ethical challenge of government surveillance is about finding the right balance between security and privacy. In an age where data is more valuable than ever, privacy has become a fundamental human right that must be protected. Governments must navigate the complex task of using surveillance to keep citizens safe without infringing on their fundamental rights to privacy and freedom.

As my *Cyberpsychology* book discusses, the impact of surveillance on mental health and behavior is significant. Knowing that one is constantly being watched can create a culture of fear and compliance, which is detrimental to both personal well-being and the health of democratic societies. Surveillance should not be about controlling or manipulating the public but about protecting the public from genuine threats.

Ethically, governments must ensure that their surveillance programs are transparent, accountable, and respectful of individual rights. Privacy should not be a casualty in the fight against terrorism or cybercrime. Instead, it should be upheld as a core value that defines the ethical boundaries of surveillance in the digital age.

The Future of Government Surveillance with Quantum Computing

Quantum computing is on the verge of transforming the landscape of digital technology and, with it, the way governments conduct surveillance. This shift will come with both advantages and new challenges, particularly in how data is collected, processed, and protected. The immense power of quantum computers has the potential to break existing cryptographic systems, allowing governments unparalleled access to encrypted data. At the same time, it also promises more robust security measures through quantum encryption technologies.

Quantum Computing: A Game-Changer for Data Surveillance

The main appeal of quantum computing lies in its ability to process massive amounts of data at speeds that classical computers cannot achieve. Classical computers work in binary, handling data in ones and zeros, which limits their ability to solve highly complex problems quickly. Quantum computers, on the other hand, use qubits, which can represent both one and zero simultaneously due to the principle of superposition. This allows quantum computers to perform calculations at exponentially faster rates than traditional machines.

For government surveillance, this means that the sheer volume of data, ranging from metadata to encrypted messages, can be processed and analyzed almost in real time. Current systems often struggle with the enormous amount of data collected from phone calls, internet traffic, and social media. However, with quantum computing, governments could potentially sift through these vast datasets with relative ease, identifying patterns and anomalies that could signify threats to national security.

Cracking Current Encryption Standards

One of the most significant implications of quantum computing for surveillance is its ability to break modern encryption methods. Current encryption techniques, such as RSA (Rivest–Shamir–Adleman) and AES (Advanced Encryption Standard), rely on the difficulty of solving complex mathematical problems, like factoring large prime numbers or performing large-scale modular arithmetic. For classical computers, these problems are incredibly time-consuming and challenging to solve, which is why RSA encryption is widely trusted to secure sensitive information.

However, quantum computers can exploit algorithms like Shor's Algorithm, which drastically reduces the time needed to factorize large numbers, making it possible to break RSA encryption. This poses a significant threat to the security of communications, financial transactions, and personal data.

Governments could use this capability to intercept and decrypt sensitive communications that were previously considered secure. In an era where encrypted messaging apps like WhatsApp, Signal, and Telegram have become the norm, quantum computing could allow state agencies to decrypt messages, emails, and other forms of private communication effortlessly. This potential raises serious concerns about privacy, civil liberties, and the extent to which individuals and organizations can protect their information.

While quantum computing threatens current encryption methods, it also presents an opportunity to develop quantum-resistant encryption, commonly known as quantum cryptography. Quantum Key Distribution (QKD) is one such method that leverages the principles of quantum mechanics to create virtually unhackable communication channels.

In QKD, encryption keys are transmitted via quantum particles, typically photons. Due to the laws of quantum mechanics, any attempt to intercept or measure these particles would immediately alter their state, making eavesdropping detectable. This promises a future where communications are not only secure from classical hacking methods but also from quantum attacks.

Governments worldwide are investing in the development of quantum cryptography to stay ahead in this digital arms race. For instance, China's Micius satellite was the first to successfully demonstrate quantum key distribution over 1,200 kilometers, proving that secure quantum communication is feasible on a global scale. Similarly, other countries, including the United States and European nations, are also racing to develop quantum networks that can protect sensitive governmental and military communications.

The challenge lies in implementing quantum cryptography on a large scale. For the foreseeable future, quantum cryptography will likely be used to protect susceptible communications, such as military, governmental, and financial data. However, as quantum technologies continue to develop, they could eventually be applied to broader surveillance and communication networks.

In addition to encryption, quantum computing will revolutionize how governments collect, store, and process data. Governments collect vast amounts of data through programs like PRISM (as seen in the U.S.) or Tempora (in the U.K.). The goal of these programs is to analyze metadata and other communication data in search of patterns that indicate criminal or terrorist activities.

The processing capabilities of classical computers limit current mass data collection systems. Sorting through enormous datasets to find meaningful information is a daunting task. The integration of AI (Artificial Intelligence) systems has improved this process by automating the detection of patterns in data. Still, AI alone cannot handle the complexity of all the information available.

Quantum computing, combined with AI, could change this. Quantum computers are uniquely suited to processing large-scale datasets that contain a high degree of complexity and interdependence. By speeding up data processing, quantum computers could allow governments to monitor communications in real time, identifying threats faster than ever before.

For instance, if a terrorist cell were coordinating attacks using encrypted messaging services, a quantum-powered surveillance system could decrypt their communications, analyze the patterns, and pinpoint their location in real time. This would allow law enforcement agencies to act quickly, potentially preventing attacks before they occur. The ability to integrate real-time data analysis with predictive capabilities using quantum computing and AI could reshape the future of intelligence gathering and surveillance.

While quantum computing offers powerful tools for government surveillance, it also poses new ethical challenges. The ability to monitor encrypted communications, process vast amounts of personal data, and track individual behaviors on a large scale raises significant concerns about civil liberties, individual rights, and democratic oversight.

1. **Loss of Privacy**: With the potential for governments to decrypt personal messages, phone calls, and even financial transactions, individuals may feel that they do not expect privacy. This leads to a chilling effect, where citizens may refrain from engaging in activities or expressing views that they believe are being monitored, even if these activities are lawful.

2. **Widespread Data Collection**: Quantum computing will enable governments to collect and store even more data than they do now. The more data collected, the higher the risk of misuse. Even with the best intentions, governments may overreach, using this data to control, manipulate, or suppress their populations. This has been particularly evident in authoritarian regimes that use surveillance technologies to silence dissent and maintain control.

3. **Bias and Discrimination**: A.I. systems already face criticism for their inherent biases, often reflecting the data they are trained on. When integrated with quantum computing, these biases could become amplified, leading to the wrongful targeting of individuals or groups. Quantum-enhanced surveillance systems might disproportionately focus on specific populations, particularly marginalized communities, under the guise of national security.

4.   **The Role of Oversight**: As surveillance technology advances, the need for effective oversight becomes more critical. Citizens must demand transparency and accountability from their governments, ensuring that surveillance powers are used responsibly and within the bounds of the law. Clear legal frameworks must be established to govern the use of quantum-powered surveillance, preventing potential abuses.

Balancing National Security and Privacy in the Quantum Era

Governments' challenge in the coming decades will be balancing quantum computing's immense capabilities with the need to protect citizens' privacy. As quantum computers become more powerful, governments will have unprecedented access to data, which can either enhance security or erode civil liberties.

One potential solution is to develop robust legal frameworks that clearly outline when and how quantum technologies can be used for surveillance. These frameworks must include strong safeguards to protect privacy, ensure transparency, and prevent misuse. International cooperation will also be crucial. Just as governments collaborate to combat global cybercrime, they will need to work together to develop ethical standards and legal agreements around the use of quantum surveillance.

Moreover, citizens must be educated about the potential implications of quantum computing and AI on their privacy. By raising awareness and advocating for digital rights, individuals can help ensure that these technologies are used responsibly.

Governments must walk a fine line, ensuring that the benefits of quantum computing are harnessed to protect national security without infringing on the fundamental rights of their citizens. The future of government surveillance with quantum computing holds immense potential, but only if used with the necessary ethical considerations and legal safeguards.

The Role of Ethics in AI and Quantum Computing

The role of ethics in artificial intelligence (AI) and quantum computing is crucial as these technologies evolve and become integrated into more aspects of society. Both AI and quantum computing hold immense potential to solve complex problems, revolutionize industries, and impact global economies. However, with such power comes responsibility. Ethical considerations must guide the development, deployment, and use of these technologies to prevent harm and ensure that they benefit all.

AI ethics is a relatively new field, emerging as AI systems become more prevalent in areas like healthcare, finance, education, and law enforcement. These systems have the potential to make decisions more quickly and accurately than humans. However, the data that trains AI systems often contains biases that reflect societal inequalities. If not carefully monitored, AI can perpetuate and even amplify these biases, leading to unfair or harmful outcomes. For example, an AI system used to screen job candidates might prioritize specific demographics over others if trained on data from a non-diverse workplace.

Similarly, facial recognition systems have been shown to perform poorly on individuals with darker skin tones, mainly because they were trained on datasets that overrepresented lighter-skinned individuals. This highlights the importance of fairness in AI systems. Developers must ensure that the data used to train AI is representative of all groups and free from biases that could lead to discriminatory outcomes. Ethical AI must focus on inclusive data collection, regular audits of training data, and the use of transparent algorithms that provide clear explanations for their decisions.

Transparency is another cornerstone of ethical AI. Many AI systems operate as "black boxes," meaning that their decision-making processes are not easily understandable, even to their creators. This opacity is particularly concerning in fields like healthcare, where AI systems might be used to recommend treatments, or in the criminal justice system, where AI might influence sentencing decisions. Users have a right to understand how and why an AI system made a particular decision, especially when those decisions have significant consequences for their lives. Ensuring that AI systems are transparent and accountable helps build trust with users and allows for the identification and correction of any errors or biases.

Privacy is also a critical ethical concern in the development of AI. AI systems often rely on vast amounts of data, much of which is personal and sensitive. This raises questions about how that data is collected, stored, and used. For example, AI systems in healthcare may analyze patients ' medical records to recommend treatments, while AI in marketing might use browsing histories to target advertisements. In both cases, users have a right to know how their data is being used and to expect that it is protected from unauthorized access. Regulations like the European Union's General Data Protection Regulation (GDPR) set important precedents by requiring organizations to ensure transparency, data protection, and accountability when using AI. Compliance with such regulations is not only a legal requirement but also an ethical obligation to safeguard individual privacy.

Quantum computing, though still in its early stages, presents a new set of ethical challenges. Quantum computers can process information at speeds far beyond those of classical computers, which opens exciting possibilities for solving complex problems. However, this also raises significant privacy and security concerns. For example, quantum computers could break current encryption methods, which are the backbone of data security on the internet. This means that sensitive information, such as personal communications, financial data, and government secrets, could become vulnerable if quantum computing is misused. Ethical quantum computing must, therefore, include the development of quantum-safe encryption methods. Researchers are already working on encryption algorithms that would remain secure even in the age of quantum computing. However, widespread adoption of these quantum-safe methods will take time, and until then, there is a significant risk of data breaches.

In addition to privacy and security concerns, quantum computing also raises issues of access and equity. Quantum computers are likely to be expensive and resource-intensive, at least in the beginning. This could lead to a concentration of quantum computing power in the hands of a few large corporations and governments, exacerbating existing inequalities. Suppose only a small group has access to this technology. In that case, they will have a disproportionate influence on its development and use, which could deepen divides between wealthy and poor nations or between large corporations and smaller competitors. Ensuring equitable access to quantum computing is an essential ethical challenge. Governments and international organizations should step in to prevent monopolies and ensure that quantum computing benefits society.

The convergence of AI and quantum computing presents even greater ethical complexities. Quantum computing could supercharge AI systems, enabling them to process even larger datasets and make faster, more accurate decisions. However, this also means that the risks associated with AI, such as bias and lack of transparency, could be amplified. Quantum-enhanced AI systems could make decisions so quickly that human oversight becomes impossible, raising concerns about accountability. Furthermore, if quantum AI systems are trained on biased data, they could perpetuate discrimination at an unprecedented scale. Developers will need to be even more vigilant in ensuring that these systems are fair, transparent, and accountable. Cross-disciplinary collaboration involving ethicists, computer scientists, social scientists, and legal experts will be critical in addressing these challenges.

Misuse of quantum computing and AI is another area that requires ethical consideration. The power of quantum computing could be harnessed for harmful purposes, such as creating more advanced hacking tools or developing autonomous weapons. This raises the need for clear ethical guidelines and international cooperation to ensure that quantum computing is used responsibly. Governments and organizations must work together to establish regulations that prevent the misuse of these technologies. Such restrictions could include bans on the use of quantum computing for offensive cyber operations or the development of autonomous weapons systems. Ethical governance will play a key role in ensuring that these powerful technologies are used to promote security and peace rather than harm individuals or societies.

Efforts are already underway to establish ethical guidelines for both AI and quantum computing. For example, the IEEE's "Ethically Aligned

Design" framework offers principles for developing AI systems that align with human values, emphasizing transparency, fairness, and accountability. Similarly, the Asilomar AI Principles, developed by researchers and ethicists, focus on ensuring that AI technologies are beneficial to humanity and that their long-term risks are carefully managed. These initiatives provide a foundation for addressing the ethical challenges of quantum computing as well.

Mitigating AI Bias in Data and Decision-Making

Bias in AI systems occurs when the algorithms, data, or processes used in the development and deployment of AI models produce outcomes that unfairly favor certain groups or individuals over others. Given the widespread use of AI in sectors such as healthcare, criminal justice, hiring, and finance, these biases can have significant real-world consequences, reinforcing existing societal inequalities and creating new forms of discrimination.

Understanding AI Bias

Bias in AI systems typically stem from one or more of the following sources:

1. **Historical Bias in Data**: AI systems learn from historical data, and if this data reflects past injustices or imbalances, the AI will replicate and possibly amplify those patterns. For example, suppose an AI system is used to predict creditworthiness but is trained on data from a financial system that has historically favored specific demographics. In that case, the AI may unfairly limit access to credit for other groups.

2. **Sampling Bias**: This occurs when the data used to train an AI system does not represent the diversity of the population it will serve. For instance, facial recognition software has been shown to be less accurate in identifying people of color, mainly Black and Asian individuals, because the training datasets were predominantly composed of images of white people.

3. **Algorithmic Bias**: Even with unbiased data, bias can emerge from the way algorithms process information. If an algorithm assigns more

weight to certain features or prioritizes specific patterns, it might systematically favor one group over another. For instance, an AI hiring tool might prioritize applicants from a particular educational background based on patterns learned from previous hiring decisions, even if those patterns don't necessarily predict job performance.

4. **Interaction Bias**: As AI systems evolve based on user interactions, they can develop biases based on those users' behavior. For example, chatbots that learn from user input might begin to replicate offensive or biased language if exposed to it frequently.

Why Is Mitigating AI Bias Important?

Addressing AI bias is critical because AI systems are increasingly being used to make decisions that affect people's lives. From healthcare diagnoses to hiring decisions and from criminal sentencing to credit approvals, biased AI systems can perpetuate inequality and unfair treatment. Mitigating bias is essential to ensure that these systems operate fairly and equitably, benefiting society rather than exacerbating existing disparities.

Ethical AI principles emphasize the need for fairness, transparency, and accountability in AI. As described in my *Cyberpsychology Book*, technology's impact on human behavior is significant, and AI systems, when biased, can affect how people are treated in both the digital and physical worlds. Therefore, AI systems must be designed and deployed with careful attention to mitigating bias at every stage of their development and operation.

1. Collecting Diverse and Representative Data

The foundation of any AI system is the data it is trained on. To mitigate bias, this data must be as diverse and representative as possible. This involves:

- **Auditing Existing Datasets**: Before an AI system is trained, developers must audit the dataset to ensure it represents the population the AI will serve. For example, suppose a healthcare AI is being developed to assist in diagnosing diseases across different demographic groups. In that case, the training data must include individuals from various racial, ethnic, and socioeconomic backgrounds.

- **Oversampling Underrepresented Groups**: When certain groups are underrepresented in the data, oversampling can help ensure that the AI does not overlook their needs. For example, in facial recognition systems, increasing the proportion of images of people of color in the training data can improve accuracy across all racial groups.

- **Balancing Historical Data**: In many cases, historical data is inherently biased. For example, suppose an AI system is being used to predict recidivism rates in the criminal justice system. In that case, it might be based on data from a justice system that has disproportionately affected certain racial groups. To mitigate this bias, developers must balance the dataset by adjusting for these historical inequities.

Incorporating such practices, as outlined in one of my books titled *Artificial Intelligence: A New Dawn,* emphasizes the importance of fairness when developing AI systems that operate on a global scale.

2. Algorithmic Fairness

Bias can emerge not just from the data but also from how the algorithm processes that data. Several approaches can be employed to ensure that algorithms themselves do not introduce or exacerbate bias:

- **Bias Testing and Auditing**: AI systems should be regularly tested for bias during the development process. This involves running simulations to see if the algorithm produces different outcomes for different demographic groups. If any biases are detected, developers can adjust the algorithm or retrain it with more representative data. This proactive approach helps identify and mitigate biases before the AI system is deployed.

- **Fairness Constraints**: Developers can also incorporate fairness constraints into the algorithm itself. These constraints ensure that the algorithm treats all groups equitably, regardless of their race, gender, or other characteristics. For example, in a hiring algorithm, fairness constraints can prevent the system from disproportionately favoring candidates from specific educational backgrounds.

- **Explainable AI (XAI)**: Explainability is a critical component of ethical AI systems. Developers must be able to explain how an AI reached its decision, especially in high-stakes scenarios such as hiring or criminal justice. Explainable AI techniques allow developers to understand and address potential sources of bias in the algorithm, ensuring that the system makes fair and justifiable decisions.

3. Human Oversight and Intervention

AI systems should not operate in isolation. Human oversight is crucial to ensure that AI decisions are fair, accurate, and free from bias. This can be achieved through:

- **Human-in-the-Loop (HITL)**: In many AI systems, humans play an essential role in overseeing and validating the AI's decisions. This is particularly important in sensitive areas such as healthcare or criminal justice, where AI-driven decisions can have life-altering consequences. Human-in-the-loop systems allow humans to intervene and override AI decisions if necessary, ensuring that the final decision is made with fairness and accountability.

- **Cross-Disciplinary Teams**: AI development should involve diverse teams with expertise in various fields, including data science, ethics, law, and sociology. This ensures that the AI system is designed with a holistic view of its potential impact on different demographic groups. By including experts from multiple disciplines, developers are more likely to recognize and address potential biases before the AI is deployed.

- **Regular Bias Audits**: Once an AI system is deployed, it should be subject to regular audits to ensure that it continues to operate fairly. These audits can reveal whether the system is producing biased outcomes over time and allow developers to adjust as needed. Regular audits are crucial in AI systems that evolve based on user interactions, as these interactions can introduce new biases into the system.

4. User-Centered Design

The design of AI systems should be user-centered, meaning that it considers the needs, experiences, and concerns of all potential users. This approach involves:

- **Engaging Diverse User Groups**: During the development process, it is essential to engage with diverse user groups to understand their needs and concerns. This ensures that the AI system is designed to serve all users equitably rather than prioritizing the needs of one group over another.

- **Inclusive Testing**: AI systems should be tested with diverse user groups before deployment to ensure that they work well for everyone. For example, in voice recognition systems, developers should test the system with users who speak different languages, have different accents, and come from various cultural backgrounds.

- **Feedback Mechanisms**: AI systems should include mechanisms for users to provide feedback on their experiences. This feedback can help developers identify potential biases and adjust the system to ensure that it operates well for all users.

5. Legal and Regulatory Compliance

To mitigate AI bias, developers must ensure that their systems comply with legal and regulatory requirements for fairness and non-discrimination. Regulations such as the General Data Protection Regulation (GDPR) in Europe and the Equal Employment Opportunity laws in the United States require that AI systems be transparent and fair. Compliance with these regulations ensures that AI systems do not produce biased outcomes and that users have recourse if they feel they have been mistreated.

In my book *Unveiling Privacy*, I emphasize the importance of compliance and regular audits in preventing privacy violations and maintaining fairness. Similarly, in AI systems, adherence to legal and ethical standards is crucial for ensuring that technology does not perpetuate or amplify biases.

Challenges in Mitigating AI Bias

While there are many strategies for mitigating bias in AI systems, several challenges remain:

- **Complexity of Bias**: Bias in AI systems is often complex and multifaceted, making it challenging to identify and eliminate. For example, an algorithm might be free of gender bias but still exhibit racial bias. Developers must take a comprehensive approach to bias mitigation, addressing all potential sources of bias in the system.

- **Evolving Bias**: AI systems that evolve based on user interactions can develop new biases. This means that bias mitigation is not a one-time process but requires ongoing monitoring and adjustment.

- **Trade-offs**: In some cases, there may be trade-offs between different types of fairness. For example, an AI system designed to be fair across gender lines may inadvertently produce biased outcomes for specific age groups. Developers must carefully balance these trade-offs to ensure that the system operates well for all users.

Ethical AI systems must be designed with fairness, transparency, and accountability in mind. Developers need to adopt a proactive approach to ethics when building these systems, ensuring that potential issues are addressed before they can cause harm.

Ethical AI Design Principles

1. **Fairness**: AI systems should be designed to treat all users fairly without discriminating based on race, gender, or other personal characteristics. This can be achieved by ensuring that the training data is representative of all groups and that the algorithm is tested for fairness before deployment.

2. **Transparency**: One of the biggest challenges with AI systems is the "black box" problem. AI makes decisions in ways that are difficult to understand or explain. Ethical AI systems must be transparent, meaning that their decision-making processes are clear and understandable to users. Developers should provide documentation and explanations of how the AI system works, what data it uses, and how it reaches its conclusions.

3. **Accountability**: In ethical AI systems, decisions must be clearly accountable. When an AI makes a mistake or causes harm, mechanisms should be in place to correct it. This includes human oversight of AI systems and ensuring that there are ways to appeal or challenge AI decisions.

4. **Privacy**: AI systems must respect user privacy and protect sensitive information. This is especially important as AI systems often handle vast amounts of personal data. Developers should implement strong

data protection measures and ensure that AI systems are compliant with privacy regulations like GDPR.

5. **Safety**: AI systems must be designed to operate safely, minimizing the risk of harm to users. This includes ensuring that AI systems are robust and secure, preventing them from being manipulated by malicious actors.

The Role of Quantum Computing in Ethical AI

Quantum computing presents new opportunities and challenges for building ethical AI systems. On one hand, quantum computers have the potential to process data at unprecedented speeds, leading to faster and more efficient AI systems. However, this same power could also be misused, leading to significant ethical concerns.

One key challenge with quantum computing is that it could break current encryption methods, making sensitive data vulnerable to attacks. Ethical quantum computing will require new approaches to data security, ensuring that personal information is protected in this new era of computing.

In addition, quantum computing could exacerbate the problem of AI bias. Since quantum computers can process much larger datasets than classical computers, they could unintentionally amplify existing biases in the data. To address this, developers will need to be even more vigilant about ensuring that their data is diverse and representative.

Ethical AI Governance

Governments and international organizations play a crucial role in establishing ethical guidelines for AI and quantum computing. Many countries have already introduced regulations that require AI systems to be transparent and fair, such as the GDPR in the European Union. These regulations are essential for ensuring that AI systems are used responsibly and do not cause harm to society.

In the future, we can expect more comprehensive governance frameworks for AI and quantum computing. These frameworks will likely include guidelines for mitigating bias, ensuring transparency, and protecting privacy. They may also include provisions for auditing AI systems to ensure that they are complying with ethical standards.

PART 4: PREPARING FOR THE FUTURE OF SECURITY AND PRIVACY

AI-DRIVEN CYBERSECURITY IN THE FUTURE

The rise of artificial intelligence (AI) has reshaped how we approach cybersecurity. In a world increasingly reliant on digital technologies, AI's role in securing sensitive information has expanded rapidly. As cyber threats become more sophisticated, AI-driven solutions have become necessary to protect data, networks, and individuals from these evolving dangers.

AI and Machine Learning Predictions for Cybersecurity

As artificial intelligence (AI) and machine learning (ML) continue to evolve, their influence on cybersecurity will become even more profound. AI's ability to process vast amounts of data and identify patterns at lightning speed has already revolutionized many areas of cybersecurity, from malware detection to real-time threat prevention. Looking to the future, AI and ML are poised to take cybersecurity to an entirely new level, offering predictive, adaptive, and autonomous solutions.

1. Predictive Threat Detection and Response

The future of cybersecurity will increasingly rely on AI and machine learning's predictive capabilities. Today, most cybersecurity solutions are reactive, responding to attacks after they happen. In contrast, AI and ML can proactively detect potential threats before they fully materialize, enabling systems to act before an attack occurs.

- **Behavioral Analysis and Anomaly Detection:**

AI systems can monitor user behavior across networks, looking for patterns that deviate from the norm. This capability allows AI to spot unusual activity that may signal a security threat. For instance, if an employee suddenly accesses sensitive files at odd hours, this could indicate a potential insider threat. AI can immediately flag this behavior, allowing security teams to investigate and respond swiftly.

In the future, this ability will become more sophisticated. AI systems will build comprehensive profiles of user behavior over time, learning what constitutes "normal" for each user. As the AI learns, it will become better at identifying subtle anomalies that humans or traditional security systems might overlook. This will dramatically reduce the time between detecting and neutralizing a threat, minimizing damage to the organization.

- **Machine Learning for Threat Prediction:**

Machine learning algorithms, which can improve their accuracy and efficiency with time and exposure to new data, will be critical players in cybersecurity prediction. In the future, machine learning systems will have access to more data points from diverse sources (such as network traffic, emails, social media activity, and more). The more data these systems analyze, the more predictive they become.

For example, a machine learning model can predict the likelihood of a new vulnerability being exploited based on past patterns and trends. By analyzing the behaviors of known attackers, ML systems can also anticipate future tactics, techniques, and procedures (TTPs) that cybercriminals may use. This information will be crucial for security teams to shore up defenses before an actual attack takes place.

Additionally, predictive AI can foresee when a particular piece of software might become vulnerable based on its age, usage patterns, and the prevalence of similar attacks in the past. Companies will be able to proactively update or patch software before attackers find and exploit vulnerabilities.

2. AI-Powered Autonomous Cyber Defense

One of the most promising developments in cybersecurity is the rise of autonomous AI-driven defense systems. Currently, cybersecurity efforts depend on human oversight and intervention, which limits how fast responses can be executed. In the future, AI will take over many of these functions, allowing systems to defend themselves automatically without waiting for human commands.

- **Autonomous Systems for Attack Mitigation:**

In the future, AI systems will be capable of fully automating the initial stages of threat detection and response. When a threat is identified, AI will isolate compromised systems, neutralize the attack, and reconfigure network settings to prevent further damage. This level of automation will reduce response times significantly, from hours or days to milliseconds. The idea is to have self-healing systems that can adapt on the fly to counter attacks in real time, significantly reducing the impact of breaches.

For instance, consider a ransomware attack in which malware begins encrypting an organization's files. Instead of waiting for IT professionals to intervene, AI can instantly detect abnormal file behavior, isolate the infected system from the rest of the network, and deploy countermeasures like rolling back the system to an earlier, uninfected state. This not only stops the ransomware but also ensures that business operations are minimally impacted.

- **AI and Cybersecurity Operations Centers (SOCs):**

Soon, AI-driven SOCs will likely become the norm. Instead of requiring large teams of human analysts to monitor network activity 24/7, these centers will be AI-managed, with human intervention only needed for the most complex or nuanced threats. These AI-driven SOCs will continuously scan for known vulnerabilities and test systems against emerging threats, freeing up human resources for more strategic initiatives.

As machine learning models are exposed to new forms of cyberattacks, they will evolve to recognize and block these attacks in real time. The goal is to create systems that not only predict and prevent attacks but also improve autonomously over time. Future AI will not only detect anomalies but also make decisions about which countermeasures to deploy, essentially functioning as cybersecurity "robots" capable of making complex defense decisions on the fly.

3. Adaptive Learning and Cybersecurity

One of AI's most promising aspects is its potential for adaptive learning. As cyber threats evolve, so must the defense mechanisms in place to stop them. The future of AI in cybersecurity lies in its ability to adapt to these changing threats autonomously.

- **Adaptive Algorithms to Counter New Threats:**

AI systems that use adaptive learning can evolve as cybercriminals develop new techniques. Instead of relying on a fixed set of rules or static algorithms, adaptive AI systems will continuously learn from each attack they encounter. For example, if a hacker uses a previously unseen method to infiltrate a network, an adaptive AI system will study the attack, learn its characteristics, and incorporate this knowledge into its defense protocols. The next time a similar attack occurs, the system will be better equipped to counter it.

This ability to evolve on the go will be critical in dealing with the next generation of cyber threats, particularly those posed by nation-state actors and sophisticated organized cybercrime groups. As these adversaries invest in advanced technologies, adaptive AI-driven cybersecurity will be the first line of defense.

- **AI and Machine Learning in Malware Detection:**

Malware is one of the most persistent and evolving threats in the cybersecurity landscape. AI and ML are already helping in malware detection by analyzing large datasets of known malware signatures and identifying new, previously unseen malware. In the future, AI's role will expand from detecting known malware to predicting the development of new variants based on historical trends and behavior patterns.

AI will also make use of advanced anomaly detection algorithms to spot unknown malware based on deviations in system behavior rather than relying on predefined signatures. For example, a sudden spike in CPU usage or unexpected data flows can signal that a system is being infected with malware. AI can immediately flag this activity and take action before the malware can do any significant damage.

4. **Enhanced User Authentication and Access Control**

AI and machine learning will also play a critical role in enhancing user authentication processes. Traditional methods of authentication, such as passwords, are quickly becoming outdated and vulnerable to attacks. AI will revolutionize this space by implementing continuous authentication based on user behavior and biometrics.

- **Behavioral Biometrics for Continuous Authentication:**

In the future, AI will continuously authenticate users based on their behavior rather than relying solely on passwords or one-time PINs. For example, AI systems can monitor how a user interacts with a keyboard (keystroke dynamics), their typing speed, how they hold a smartphone, or how they move a mouse. These behavioral biometrics provide unique data points that can verify a user's identity in real time.

If a user's behavior suddenly changes, perhaps they are typing slower than usual or using different mouse patterns. AI can detect this anomaly and request further authentication, locking down the system if necessary. This continuous authentication provides a more secure and seamless experience for users, reducing the likelihood of unauthorized access.

Quantum Computing's Role in the Future of Data Protection

While AI is transforming how we defend against cyber threats, quantum computing is set to revolutionize the very foundations of data security. Quantum computing harnesses the power of quantum mechanics to solve problems that are intractable for classical computers, including some of the most complex challenges in cryptography and data protection.

1. Quantum Computing and the End of Traditional Encryption

The most significant impact of quantum computing on cybersecurity is in encryption. Today, encryption algorithms such as RSA and ECC (Elliptic Curve Cryptography) protect sensitive data across industries, from banking and finance to government and healthcare. These algorithms rely on complex mathematical problems, like factoring large numbers, which are practically impossible for classical computers to solve within a reasonable time frame.

Breaking Classical Encryption:

However, quantum computers could change this paradigm. Quantum computers leverage quantum bits (qubits) to perform computations at speeds far beyond what classical computers are capable of. Shor's algorithm, a quantum algorithm, can solve the factoring problem exponentially faster than classical algorithms. This means that a sufficiently powerful quantum computer could break RSA encryption in minutes or even seconds, rendering much of today's internet security infrastructure obsolete.

The implications of this are profound. Sensitive data that is currently secure could suddenly become vulnerable to quantum-powered attacks. Hackers using quantum computers could break into encrypted communications, steal financial data, or compromise classified government information. Therefore, organizations need to begin preparing for a post-quantum world by transitioning to quantum-resistant encryption algorithms.

2. The Rise of Quantum-Resistant Cryptography

Recognizing the threat that quantum computing poses to traditional encryption, researchers are already developing new cryptographic algorithms designed to withstand quantum attacks. These quantum-resistant algorithms are based on mathematical problems that even quantum computers cannot solve efficiently.

Lattice-Based Cryptography:

One of the most promising areas of quantum-resistant cryptography is lattice-based cryptography. Unlike RSA or ECC, which rely on number theory, lattice-based cryptography is based on problems involving high-dimensional grids (lattices). These problems are believed to be resistant to attacks by both classical and quantum computers, making them ideal candidates for securing data in the quantum era.

In the future, quantum-resistant encryption will become the standard for protecting sensitive information. Governments, financial institutions, and tech companies will need to adopt these new encryption methods to ensure that their data remains secure in a world where quantum computers are operational.

3. Quantum Key Distribution (QKD)

One of the most exciting innovations that quantum computing brings to the table is Quantum Key Distribution (QKD). QKD uses the principles of quantum mechanics to distribute encryption keys securely between two parties. This method is fundamentally different from traditional essential distribution techniques because any attempt to eavesdrop on the communication will disrupt the quantum state, immediately alerting the parties involved.

How QKD Works:

In QKD, two parties use photons (quantum particles of light) to transmit encryption keys. These photons are sent over a fiber optic cable or through free space. Due to the quantum properties of photons, any interception of the key alters the quantum state of the particles, making eavesdropping detectable. If the key is intercepted or tampered with, the communication is aborted, ensuring that the key is never compromised.

QKD is already being tested in various industries, and it has the potential to revolutionize how encryption keys are shared securely. As quantum computing continues to advance, QKD will likely become a critical tool for ensuring the confidentiality of communications in industries that handle sensitive data, such as finance, healthcare, and national security.

4. The Role of Quantum Algorithms in Cybersecurity

Beyond encryption, quantum algorithms will also enhance cybersecurity in other areas. For example, Grover's algorithm, another quantum algorithm, can significantly speed up search operations. This could improve data searching and analysis for cybersecurity purposes, allowing for faster identification of vulnerabilities or anomalies in massive datasets.

Quantum Computing and AI Synergy:

Quantum computing will also work in tandem with AI to strengthen cybersecurity. While classical AI systems are already effective at detecting and responding to threats, the power of quantum computing could take this to the next level. For example, quantum-enhanced AI systems could analyze enormous amounts of data at unprecedented speeds, improving the ability to detect subtle patterns that indicate a cyberattack.

Moreover, quantum computing could enable more advanced AI algorithms that are too complex for classical computers to handle. These algorithms could improve the prediction of cyberattacks, the simulation of potential threats, and the optimization of cybersecurity strategies. This synergy between AI and quantum computing will define the next era of cybersecurity innovation.

5. Preparing for the Quantum Threat

The emergence of quantum computing presents both opportunities and challenges for cybersecurity. While quantum computing offers exciting possibilities for improving data protection, it also introduces new risks. As quantum computers become more powerful, organizations must prepare for the potential threat to existing encryption systems.

Transitioning to Post-Quantum Cryptography:

Organizations need to begin transitioning to post-quantum cryptography now to stay ahead of quantum threats. This means adopting quantum-resistant encryption algorithms and implementing security measures like

QKD where possible. Governments and regulatory bodies will also play a critical role in driving the adoption of quantum-safe technologies across industries.

As we look to the future, quantum computing will clearly play a pivotal role in the evolution of cybersecurity. By combining the power of quantum mechanics with AI and machine learning, we can build stronger, more resilient security systems that will protect our digital infrastructure for generations to come.

How Biometrics and Ai Will Define Future Security Systems

In an era where cybersecurity threats are increasing in complexity, traditional forms of user authentication, such as passwords and PINs, are proving inadequate to protect critical systems and sensitive data. Biometrics, which refers to using physical or behavioral characteristics to authenticate individuals, has emerged as a more secure alternative. When paired with artificial intelligence (AI), biometric systems become even more powerful, allowing for more accurate, efficient, and safe methods of authentication. As we move into the future, biometrics and AI will play an increasingly crucial role in defining and shaping security systems, particularly in sectors that handle sensitive information like healthcare, finance, and government.

AI-Enhanced Biometric Authentication

Biometric security systems have gained significant traction in recent years, primarily due to their ability to provide a higher level of security than traditional authentication methods. Biometric data, such as fingerprints, facial recognition, voice patterns, and even iris scans, are unique to everyone, making them much more challenging to duplicate or steal compared to passwords, which can be easily hacked or forgotten.

However, biometric systems are not without challenges. Factors such as lighting, camera quality, or even changes in a person's appearance can affect the accuracy of facial recognition systems. At the same time, fingerprint scanners may struggle to identify individuals with wet or damaged fingers. This is where AI steps in. By incorporating machine learning algorithms into biometric systems, AI can analyze biometric data more accurately and adaptively. AI systems can "learn" from each interaction, improving the system's ability to recognize individuals, even in suboptimal conditions.

For example, facial recognition systems powered by AI are becoming increasingly adept at distinguishing between legitimate users and impostors. They can account for variations in lighting, angles, and even facial expressions, significantly reducing the number of false positives and false negatives. Additionally, AI can continuously monitor biometric data, detecting subtle changes in behavior or appearance that might indicate an imposter is trying to gain access.

The benefits of AI-driven biometric authentication are already being seen in many industries. For instance, airports are implementing AI-powered facial recognition systems to verify passengers' identities quickly and accurately. These systems compare the biometric data captured at security checkpoints with data stored in passport databases, ensuring that only authorized individuals can pass through. In the future, such systems will become even more prevalent, securing entry into not only physical locations but also digital environments such as banking systems, corporate networks, and government databases.

Biometrics and AI in Multi-Factor Authentication (MFA)

Multi-factor authentication (MFA) has become a standard in cybersecurity, combining multiple methods of verifying a user's identity. Traditionally, MFA involves something the user knows (like a password), something the user has (like a security token), and something the user is (biometric data). AI enhances this process by making it more seamless and secure.

AI can analyze multiple biometric markers in real time, such as combining voice recognition with facial recognition, to authenticate users more securely. By cross-referencing these data points, AI systems can ensure that even if one form of biometric data is compromised, the other methods will provide a second layer of defense. This adaptive approach minimizes the chances of unauthorized access while still allowing for quick and convenient logins for legitimate users.

Furthermore, AI's ability to analyze behavioral biometrics, such as the way a person types on a keyboard, their walking gait, or even how they swipe on a touchscreen, adds a layer of security. These behavioral patterns are challenging to replicate, making them an excellent complement to traditional biometric data like fingerprints or facial features. In the future, AI will likely analyze a combination of static biometrics (like fingerprints) and dynamic biometrics (like behavioral patterns) to create a comprehensive and highly secure authentication process.

This fusion of biometric and behavioral data, analyzed by AI in real-time, will become a cornerstone of MFA systems, particularly in high-security environments such as military facilities, corporate offices, and financial institutions. By leveraging AI's analytical power, these systems will provide a more robust defense against potential intruders while minimizing user friction.

The Role of AI in Improving Biometric System Accuracy and Speed

One of the critical challenges facing biometric systems today is the potential for false positives (where the system mistakenly grants access to an unauthorized user) or false negatives (where the system denies access to a legitimate user). These errors can significantly undermine the effectiveness of biometric security, particularly in environments where precision is critical.

AI helps overcome these challenges by continuously improving the accuracy and speed of biometric systems. Machine learning algorithms can be trained on vast datasets of biometric information, allowing the system to refine its pattern recognition capabilities over time. As more data is fed into the system, the AI becomes better at identifying subtle differences in biometric markers, reducing the likelihood of errors.

For instance, in facial recognition systems, AI can analyze millions of facial images to "learn" the nuances of human features. This enables the system to identify individuals even when they are wearing glasses, have grown a beard, or are in low-light conditions. In fingerprint scanning systems, AI can analyze the minutiae of a fingerprint and match it to stored data with incredible precision, even if the finger is slightly damaged or dirty.

Additionally, AI-powered biometric systems are becoming faster. In environments where speed is critical, such as airport security checkpoints or large-scale events, AI can process biometric data in real time, allowing for rapid authentication without compromising security. This speed and accuracy make AI-driven biometric systems ideal for high-traffic areas where security must be both efficient and reliable.

Biometric Data Privacy and Security: A Critical Challenge

While biometric systems offer enhanced security, they also raise significant privacy concerns. Unlike passwords, biometric data cannot be changed if compromised. If a hacker manages to steal someone's biometric data, such as their fingerprint or facial scan, the implications can be far-reaching. Unlike a password, which can be reset, biometric traits are permanent, making it essential to ensure that this data is stored and transmitted securely.

AI plays a crucial role in protecting biometric data from unauthorized access. Advanced encryption techniques powered by AI ensure that biometric data is securely stored and transmitted. AI can also be used to detect anomalies in biometric data use, such as multiple access attempts from different locations or unusual usage patterns, which might indicate that a user's biometric data has been compromised.

Moreover, AI can enable biometric systems to operate decentralized, reducing the need for large databases of biometric data that could become targets for hackers. In decentralized systems, biometric data is stored locally on the user's device, and AI algorithms process the data without ever transmitting it to a central server. This approach not only enhances privacy but also reduces the potential for large-scale data breaches.

However, even with these protections, biometric systems must comply with stringent privacy regulations, such as the General Data Protection Regulation (GDPR) in the European Union, which sets strict guidelines for the collection, storage, and use of personal data, including biometric information. As AI-driven biometric systems become more widespread, organizations must ensure that they implement robust security measures to protect biometric data while complying with privacy laws.

The Future of AI and Biometrics: Beyond Authentication

While biometrics are currently used primarily for authentication, the future of AI-driven biometric systems extends far beyond verifying user identities. AI's ability to analyze biometric data in real time opens new possibilities for using biometrics in a variety of applications.

1. Health Monitoring

One of the most exciting future applications of AI and biometrics is in healthcare. AI can analyze biometric data, such as heart rate, skin temperature, and oxygen levels, to monitor an individual's health in real time. This data can be used to detect early signs of illness, track chronic conditions, or even predict medical emergencies before they occur.

In the workplace, AI-driven biometric systems could monitor employees' health and well-being, ensuring that they are not exposed to dangerous working conditions or health risks. For instance, biometric sensors could monitor a worker's vital signs during a physically demanding task, alerting supervisors if there is a risk of injury or exhaustion.

2. Personalized Security Systems

As AI and biometric technologies continue to evolve, security systems will become increasingly personalized. Rather than relying on a single biometric marker, such as a fingerprint or facial scan, future systems will combine multiple forms of biometric data, including behavioral biometrics like voice patterns or typing rhythms, to create a unique profile for each user.

These personalized security systems will adapt over time, learning from the user's behavior and adjusting as needed. For example, if a user's voice changes due to illness or aging, the AI system will be able to adapt to these changes without requiring the user to re-enroll in the system. This continuous learning process will ensure that biometric systems remain accurate and reliable, even as users' biometric data evolves.

3. Seamless Integration with IoT Devices

In the future, AI-driven biometric systems will be integrated with the Internet of Things (IoT), allowing for seamless authentication across multiple devices. For example, a user's biometric data could be used to unlock their smartphone, car, and home security system, all without the need for passwords or PINs.

AI will manage the authentication process, ensuring that only authorized users can access connected devices. This level of integration will make biometric security systems more convenient and efficient while also enhancing security by eliminating the need for multiple, potentially insecure, authentication methods.

4. Biometrics in National Security and Law Enforcement

AI-driven biometric systems will also play a significant role in national security and law enforcement. Governments are already using facial recognition systems to monitor public spaces and identify individuals involved in criminal activities. In the future, AI will enhance these systems, allowing for real-time identification and tracking of individuals across multiple locations.

However, the widespread use of biometrics in law enforcement raises critical ethical questions about privacy and surveillance. As AI-driven biometric systems become more advanced, it will be essential to strike a balance between enhancing security and protecting individual privacy rights.

Biometrics and AI as the Future of Security

The integration of AI and biometrics will define the future of security. AI will enhance the accuracy, efficiency, and protection of biometric systems, making them more reliable and adaptable to the evolving cybersecurity landscape. At the same time, biometric systems will provide the next generation of user authentication, offering a more secure alternative to traditional passwords and PINs.

However, as AI-driven biometric systems become more widespread, it will be essential to address the privacy and ethical challenges they present. Organizations must implement robust security measures to protect biometric data and ensure compliance with privacy regulations. Additionally, as biometric systems move beyond authentication and into areas like healthcare and national security, it will be essential to consider the broader implications of these technologies for privacy, security, and individual rights.

The future of biometrics and AI is bright, offering new possibilities for securing our digital and physical worlds. By combining the power of AI with the uniqueness of biometric data, we can create security systems that are not only more secure but also more convenient and user-friendly, paving the way for a safer and more connected future.

QUANTUM ENCRYPTION AND CYBERSECURITY

As the world becomes more connected through the internet, cybersecurity has become a critical aspect of our daily lives. From banking and shopping online to storing sensitive personal and business data, our reliance on the internet exposes us to various cyber threats. While current encryption methods do an excellent job of protecting our data, they might not be sufficient in the future. This is where quantum encryption comes into play, offering a new way to secure our communication channels and sensitive information.

Quantum Encryption: The Future of Secure Communication

In the ever-evolving world of cybersecurity, protecting communication from prying eyes is more critical than ever. With cyberattacks becoming more sophisticated, encryption, one of the most relied-upon methods of securing digital communication, faces increasing challenges. As discussed in my *Artificial Intelligence: A New Dawn* and the *Unveiling Privacy book*, current encryption standards, such as RSA and AES, rely on complex mathematical problems that would take traditional computers thousands, if not millions, of years to solve. However, with the rapid development of quantum computing, these encryption methods may soon be rendered obsolete. This brings us to quantum encryption, which holds the key to securing communication in the quantum age.

The Limitations of Classical Encryption

To fully appreciate the power of quantum encryption, it's essential to understand the vulnerabilities of classical encryption methods. Traditional encryption relies on the difficulty of solving specific mathematical problems, such as factoring large prime numbers (in the case of RSA) or solving discrete logarithms (in the case of elliptic curve cryptography). These problems are challenging for classical computers to solve, providing a solid layer of security.

However, the emergence of quantum computers threatens to break these cryptographic systems. Unlike classical computers, which use bits as their basic unit of information (either a 0 or a 1), quantum computers use qubits, which can exist in multiple states simultaneously due to a property called superposition. This allows quantum computers to perform many calculations at once, making them exponentially faster at solving certain types of problems.

One of the biggest threats posed by quantum computers is Shor's algorithm, which can factor large numbers exponentially faster than the best classical algorithms. This means that once quantum computers reach a certain level of maturity, they will be able to break RSA encryption, which underpins much of today's secure communications. As *Artificial Intelligence: A New Dawn* points out, this could lead to a security crisis, as encrypted data transmitted today could potentially be decrypted by quantum computers in the future, exposing sensitive information retroactively.

This is where quantum encryption enters the scene as the next frontier in secure communication.

How Quantum Encryption Works

Quantum encryption leverages the principles of quantum mechanics to create security mechanisms that are fundamentally more secure than classical encryption. One of the most essential methods is quantum key distribution (QKD). Unlike classical encryption, which uses mathematical algorithms to generate encryption keys, QKD uses the laws of quantum physics to create and share encryption keys between two parties.

In QKD, encryption keys are generated using qubits, and the key exchange process is conducted through quantum communication channels, such as optical fibers or even satellite links. The unique aspect of QKD lies in its reliance on the Heisenberg Uncertainty Principle, which states that it is impossible to measure a quantum system without disturbing it. This means that if an eavesdropper tries to intercept the quantum key, it will inevitably disturb the quantum state of the particles, which will alert the sender and receiver to the intrusion.

For example, imagine a scenario where Alice wants to send a secure message to Bob. Using QKD, Alice generates a quantum key that is encoded in the polarization states of photons. These photons are then sent to Bob through a quantum channel. Suppose an eavesdropper (commonly referred to as Eve) tries to intercept the key by measuring the photons' polarization. In that case, the act of measuring will disturb their quantum states, making it evident that the communication has been compromised. Alice and Bob can then discard the compromised key and generate a new one, ensuring that only they have access to the secure key.

Because any attempt to eavesdrop on the quantum key distribution will be detected, QKD offers an unprecedented level of communication security. Unlike classical encryption, which can theoretically be broken given enough computational power, quantum encryption is provably secure because it is rooted in the fundamental laws of physics. This makes it especially attractive for applications that require the highest levels of security, such as government communications, financial transactions, and military operations.

Real-World Applications of Quantum Encryption

Quantum encryption is no longer a theoretical concept; it is already being implemented in real-world scenarios. Countries like China, the United States, and several European nations are investing heavily in quantum encryption research and development. China has made significant strides in this area, launching the world's first quantum communications satellite,

Micius, in 2016. The satellite successfully demonstrated long-distance QKD, providing a secure communication channel between ground stations thousands of kilometers apart.

Additionally, financial institutions are beginning to explore the use of quantum encryption to secure transactions and protect customer data. The Swiss banking industry, for example, has piloted quantum encryption systems to secure sensitive data transmitted between financial institutions. With quantum encryption, banks can ensure that their communications are secure from even the most advanced cyber threats, providing peace of mind for their clients and regulators alike.

Governments are also recognizing the potential of quantum encryption for securing diplomatic communications and protecting national security. In a world where cyber espionage is on the rise, the ability to secure sensitive diplomatic messages and military communications from interception is crucial. The adoption of quantum encryption by government agencies will likely grow in the coming years as quantum computers become more powerful and the threat to classical encryption increases.

Challenges and Limitations of Quantum Encryption

While quantum encryption offers unparalleled security, it is not without its challenges. One of the biggest obstacles to widespread adoption is the infrastructure required to support quantum communication. Quantum encryption relies on specialized equipment, such as photon detectors and quantum repeaters, which are not yet widely available. Additionally, quantum communication channels, like optical fibers, are limited by distance, as the signal weakens over long distances. This is where satellite-based QKD, like China's Micius, could provide a solution, but building and launching quantum satellites is an expensive and complex endeavor.

Another challenge is **cost**. Currently, quantum encryption systems are expensive to implement and maintain, making them accessible primarily to governments and large corporations. For quantum encryption to become more widely used, costs will need to come down, and the technology will need to become more scalable.

However, as with many emerging technologies, these challenges are likely to be overcome with time. As quantum encryption continues to be developed and tested, its applications will expand, and its costs will decrease, making it more accessible to a broader range of users.

Preventing Identity Theft and Fraud with Quantum Systems

Identity theft and fraud are among the most pervasive and damaging forms of cybercrime in the modern digital landscape. Criminals use stolen personal information to commit a wide range of fraudulent activities, from opening credit cards in someone else's name to siphoning money from bank accounts. The *Unveiling Privacy* and *Zero Trust books* highlight that traditional cybersecurity measures, such as password protection and two-factor authentication, have proven to be insufficient in altogether preventing these crimes.

As cybercriminals become more sophisticated, quantum encryption offers a promising solution for preventing identity theft and fraud. By providing a level of security that is far beyond what classical encryption can offer, quantum systems can help protect personal information and prevent it from falling into the wrong hands.

How Identity Theft Happens Today

Before delving into how quantum systems can help prevent identity theft, it is essential to understand how identity theft typically occurs today. Cybercriminals use a variety of techniques to steal personal information, including:

1. **Phishing**: Fraudsters send fake emails or messages that appear to be from legitimate sources, such as banks or government agencies, to trick individuals into revealing sensitive information, such as passwords, social security numbers, or credit card details.

2. **Data Breaches**: Hackers target companies and organizations that store large amounts of personal data, such as retailers, hospitals, or credit bureaus. Once they breach these systems, they can steal millions of records containing personal information.

3. **Malware**: Cybercriminals use malware (malicious software) to infect computers and steal personal information directly from users. This can include keyloggers that capture every keystroke or spyware that monitors a victim's online activity.

4. **Account Takeover**: Criminals use stolen credentials to take over someone's online accounts, such as email, social media, or banking accounts. Once they gain access, they can impersonate the victim, steal funds, or further compromise their identity.

Traditional defenses, such as firewalls, antivirus software, and encryption, provide some protection, but they are not foolproof. As highlighted in my *Zero Trust* book, the best approach to cybersecurity is to assume that no one, not even those within an organization's network, can be fully trusted. This philosophy underpins the concept of Zero-Trust security, which limits access to sensitive data and continuously verifies users' identities.

Quantum Encryption for Identity Protection

Quantum encryption offers several advantages over classical encryption when it comes to protecting personal information. As we discussed earlier, quantum key distribution (QKD) ensures that encryption keys cannot be intercepted without detection. This makes quantum encryption particularly effective at securing the transmission of sensitive personal data, such as social security numbers, credit card information, or biometric data.

For example, imagine you are applying for a loan online. You enter your personal information, including your social security number, into the bank's website. With traditional encryption, this information is scrambled and transmitted over the internet, but a sophisticated hacker could intercept it. With quantum encryption, however, the information is protected by quantum keys, making it virtually impossible for the hacker to steal the data without being detected.

Beyond securing data transmission, quantum encryption can also help verify identities. As discussed in my *Cyberpsychology* book, the increasing use of biometric data such as fingerprints, facial recognition, and retinal scans presents new opportunities for securing identities. However, biometric data is susceptible, and if stolen, it cannot be changed like a password.

Quantum encryption can protect biometric data by ensuring that it is encrypted with quantum-secure keys, making it far more difficult for cybercriminals to steal or misuse. In addition, quantum-based authentication systems can verify a person's identity in real time, ensuring that only authorized individuals can access specific systems or accounts. This could be particularly useful in industries such as banking or healthcare, where unauthorized access to sensitive personal information can have devastating consequences.

Quantum-Based Fraud Prevention

In addition to preventing identity theft, quantum systems can also combat fraud. Quantum encryption can secure financial transactions, ensuring that they are not intercepted or altered by fraudsters. For instance, a credit card transaction encrypted with quantum keys would be much more difficult to hack than one protected by classical encryption methods.

Quantum systems can also help prevent fraud through quantum-based digital signatures. A digital signature is a way of verifying the authenticity and integrity of a message or document. With classical digital signatures, it is possible (though very difficult) for a hacker to forge a signature or alter a document without being detected. However, quantum digital signatures offer a much higher level of security because they rely on the principles of quantum mechanics. Any attempt to alter or forge a quantum digital signature would immediately become apparent, making it much more difficult for fraudsters to carry out their schemes.

In the context of online banking, for example, quantum-based digital signatures could be used to verify that the account holder authorized a transaction and that the details of the transaction (such as the amount and recipient) were not altered. If someone attempted to alter the transaction in any way, the quantum signature would be invalidated, preventing the fraudulent transaction from going through.

Another promising application of quantum systems in fraud prevention is the development of quantum-secure blockchains. Blockchain technology, which underpins cryptocurrencies like Bitcoin, relies on cryptographic methods to ensure the security and integrity of the data stored in the blockchain. However, as quantum computers become more powerful, there is a risk that they could break the cryptographic algorithms used in traditional blockchains, leading to security vulnerabilities.

To address this, researchers are exploring the use of quantum encryption to create quantum-resistant blockchains, which would be secure against attacks by quantum computers. Integrating quantum encryption into blockchain systems makes it possible to create an unbreakable chain of trust, ensuring that transactions and records stored in the blockchain cannot be tampered with by fraudsters.

Addressing Ethical Challenges in Quantum Cryptography

Quantum cryptography promises to revolutionize the way we think about cybersecurity, offering unprecedented security and protection against even the most sophisticated cyber threats. However, like any groundbreaking technology, it also brings a set of ethical challenges that need careful consideration. While quantum encryption holds enormous potential for securing sensitive communications and protecting against identity theft and fraud, it also introduces complex dilemmas that must be addressed if we are to create a future where privacy and security coexist harmoniously.

1. The Ethical Divide: Widening the Gap

One of the most prominent concerns with quantum cryptography is the potential for it to widen the gap between the haves and the have-nots. As you explored in my *Unveiling Privacy* and *Cyberpsychology* books, technology has the power to create disparities between those who can afford it and those who cannot. Quantum encryption, being a high-tech solution, is likely to be adopted first by governments, large corporations, and wealthy individuals. Smaller businesses, less affluent individuals, and even some nations may struggle to access the technology, leading to a digital divide where only a select few are truly secure.

This exclusivity could have severe implications for global cybersecurity. Imagine a world where powerful entities such as multinational corporations or governments enjoy the benefits of quantum encryption. At the same time, smaller organizations and everyday citizens continue to rely on traditional encryption methods that quantum computers can easily break. This imbalance could leave millions vulnerable to cyberattacks while only the most privileged enjoy proper protection.

To address this ethical challenge, there must be a concerted effort to democratize quantum encryption. Much like the development of internet infrastructure, there should be initiatives to ensure that quantum cryptography becomes accessible to all, not just the wealthy or powerful. Governments and international bodies will need to invest in programs that promote the equitable distribution of this technology, helping to level the playing field in terms of cybersecurity. Otherwise, we risk exacerbating existing inequalities in the digital realm, creating a world where only a privileged few can protect themselves from the cyber threats of tomorrow.

2. Data Privacy: The Ethics of Enhanced Surveillance

As you have explored in the *Privacy* book, one of the core concerns of modern cybersecurity is data privacy. Quantum encryption, while providing powerful security tools, also presents new challenges in this area. The reason is simple: as quantum cryptography becomes more advanced, it enables the collection and encryption of massive amounts of data. This presents a significant ethical dilemma: *who controls the data?* And more importantly, how do we ensure that quantum encryption is not used as a tool for mass surveillance?

Quantum encryption, primarily when used by governments and corporations, could lead to a future where vast quantities of data are encrypted and stored securely, potentially forever. This could create a scenario where individuals' private information, communications, and even movements are constantly monitored, encrypted, and stored by large entities. While this data may be secure from cybercriminals, it raises serious questions about privacy and the right to be forgotten. Once encrypted, data can be preserved indefinitely, making it difficult, if not impossible, to delete or remove.

This leads to another ethical question: what happens to the right to privacy when data is stored indefinitely? Will individuals lose control over their personal information as quantum encryption becomes more widespread? These are crucial issues that need to be addressed, particularly as governments and corporations are likely to adopt quantum cryptography long before individuals do.

One potential solution to this challenge is to establish strict regulations around data retention and encryption practices. Laws could mandate that encrypted data be stored for limited periods, ensuring that individuals retain the right to delete or remove their information from digital databases. Governments must also ensure that quantum encryption is not used as a tool for mass surveillance and that individuals' privacy rights are respected, even as cybersecurity technologies evolve.

3. Quantum Cryptography and Regulatory Oversight

Another significant ethical challenge surrounding quantum cryptography is the question of regulatory oversight. Quantum encryption is a powerful tool, but without proper regulation, it could harm society. For instance, if certain countries or corporations adopt quantum encryption without international cooperation, they could use the technology to protect illegal activities, evade law enforcement, or even engage in cyber warfare.

Without regulation, quantum encryption could become a double-edged sword. While it would protect legitimate communications and prevent cyberattacks, it could also shield criminals and terrorists from being tracked by authorities. Quantum encryption could, for example, be used by organized crime syndicates or terrorist organizations to hide their communications from law enforcement agencies, creating a haven for illicit activities.

To prevent this, international cooperation will be critical in developing regulatory frameworks that govern the use of quantum encryption. Nations will need to work together to create laws and treaties that prevent the misuse of quantum cryptography while still allowing its legitimate use for cybersecurity. This will require balancing the right to privacy with the need for security, ensuring that individuals and organizations can protect themselves without giving criminals and bad actors free rein to operate without oversight.

Regulatory bodies should also focus on establishing ethical standards for quantum cryptography. These standards would ensure that quantum encryption is used in a way that benefits society rather than being exploited for personal or corporate gain. Ethical guidelines include ensuring that quantum encryption is not used to undermine human rights, protecting whistleblowers and journalists from government surveillance, and ensuring that individuals retain control over their data.

4. AI and Quantum Cryptography: The Ethics of Autonomy

Quantum encryption also raises ethical concerns when it intersects with artificial intelligence (AI). As explored in my *Artificial Intelligence: A New Dawn* and *Cyberpsychology* books, AI plays an increasingly important role in cybersecurity, helping to identify threats, secure networks, and even manage encryption processes. However, when AI manages quantum encryption, new ethical challenges arise, particularly around the issue of autonomy.

AI-driven quantum cryptography systems may one day be capable of making decisions about what data to encrypt when to encrypt it, and how to respond to potential threats. This raises questions about how much control humans should have over these systems. For instance, if an AI system decides to encrypt certain communications without human input, who is responsible for that decision? And what happens if the AI makes a mistake, encrypting sensitive data that should have been made available to law enforcement or regulatory bodies?

There is also the question of accountability. If AI systems are given the authority to manage quantum encryption, how do we ensure that these systems act in ways that align with ethical principles? What if an AI system designed to prioritize security ends up infringing on individuals' privacy rights by over-encrypting data? These are complex questions that need to be addressed as AI and quantum cryptography become more intertwined.

One potential solution is to ensure that human oversight remains a crucial component of any AI-driven quantum cryptography system. While AI can help automate encryption processes, human operators should always have the final say in critical decisions. This would ensure that AI systems remain tools to assist humans rather than autonomous agents capable of making ethical decisions on their own.

5. The International Ethics of Quantum Cryptography

Finally, there is the ethical challenge of ensuring that quantum cryptography is used for the global good rather than becoming a tool of geopolitical power. As mentioned in my *Zero Trust book*, cybersecurity is increasingly becoming an international issue, with cyberattacks often crossing national borders. Quantum cryptography will undoubtedly become a tool of statecraft, with countries investing heavily in quantum encryption to protect their national interests.

However, this raises ethical concerns about how quantum cryptography will be used in international relations. Will countries use quantum encryption to spy on one another or to protect their intelligence agencies from foreign surveillance? Will quantum cryptography become part of the cyber arms race, with nations competing to develop the most advanced quantum encryption tools? These are real concerns that must be addressed through international dialogue and cooperation.

Countries will need to work together to establish global norms for quantum cryptography's use to prevent its misuse. This could involve the creation of international treaties that limit the use of quantum encryption for espionage or cyber warfare and agreements on how to share it for peaceful purposes.

In addition, the United Nations and other international organizations could regulate the use of quantum cryptography, ensuring that it is used in ways that promote global security and peace. By working together, nations can help prevent the rise of a new cyber arms race and ensure that quantum cryptography is used to protect, rather than destabilize, the world.

CONCLUSION: THE FUTURE OF AI, QUANTUM COMPUTING, AND DATA PRIVACY

DIGITAL KEY AND LOCK

As the digital landscape continues to evolve, the convergence of artificial intelligence (AI) and quantum computing is creating new opportunities and challenges, particularly in the realm of privacy and security. Both technologies have the potential to reshape our world radically. AI is increasingly being used to optimize processes and make predictions based on vast amounts of data, while quantum computing promises to bring about breakthroughs in computational power that were previously unimaginable.

While these technologies offer numerous benefits, they also raise serious concerns about data privacy. In this era, where personal information is constantly being collected, analyzed, and stored, the stakes are higher than ever before. Protecting privacy in the age of AI and quantum computing will require new strategies, innovative technologies, and robust legal frameworks. This conclusion will explore the implications of these advancements and offer strategies for ensuring that privacy remains a fundamental right in the digital age.

The Growing Influence of Artificial Intelligence

AI is already embedded in many aspects of our lives, from the algorithms that recommend what we should watch or buy to complex systems that monitor public health, track environmental changes, and predict economic trends. The power of AI lies in its ability to process and analyze massive datasets, identifying patterns that humans might not see. This has led to significant advancements in areas such as healthcare, where AI systems are used to diagnose diseases and personalize treatments, and cybersecurity, where AI helps to detect and respond to threats in real time.

However, the increasing reliance on AI systems has led to growing concerns about how personal data is being used and protected. AI systems require vast amounts of data to function effectively, and this data often includes sensitive information such as personal habits, medical histories, financial records, and even biometric details. As AI systems become more integrated into our daily lives, the potential for misuse or unauthorized access to personal data increases.

One of the critical challenges with AI is the "black box" nature of many of its algorithms. In many cases, it isn't easy to understand how AI systems reach their decisions or conclusions. This lack of transparency can lead to issues of trust and accountability. For example, if an AI system denies a loan application or recommends a medical procedure, it can be challenging to explain why the system made that decision. This lack of clarity becomes even more problematic when sensitive personal data is involved.

To address these challenges, it is essential to develop AI systems that prioritize privacy and transparency. Techniques such as federated learning, where AI models are trained across multiple devices without transferring data to a central server, offer promising solutions for reducing the amount of personal data collected and processed by AI systems. By keeping data local and focusing on aggregated insights, federated learning can help protect individual privacy while still allowing AI systems to function effectively.

Quantum Computing: A Double-Edged Sword for Privacy

While AI is already transforming the way we interact with technology, quantum computing is set to revolutionize the very foundations of cybersecurity and data privacy. Quantum computing operates on principles that are fundamentally different from classical computing. Instead of using bits that represent either a 0 or a 1, quantum computers use qubits, which can exist in multiple states simultaneously. This allows quantum computers to perform calculations at speeds that are orders of magnitude faster than today's most powerful supercomputers.

One of the most significant implications of quantum computing is its potential to break current encryption methods. Modern encryption techniques, such as RSA and elliptic curve cryptography, rely on the difficulty of factoring large prime numbers. This task is time-consuming and computationally expensive for classical computers. However, quantum computers could solve these problems in a fraction of the time, rendering current encryption methods obsolete.

This poses a significant risk to data security. Encryption is the cornerstone of modern cybersecurity, protecting everything from online banking transactions to sensitive government communications. If quantum computers can easily break these encryption methods, then vast amounts of sensitive data could be at risk of exposure. This includes not only current data but also any encrypted data that is being stored for future use.

However, quantum computing also offers opportunities to enhance security. Quantum encryption techniques, such as quantum key distribution (QKD), are nearly unbreakable. QKD allows two parties to share a cryptographic key in such a way that any attempt to intercept or eavesdrop on the key would be immediately detected. This makes quantum encryption a promising solution for securing sensitive data in the quantum age.

The challenge lies in the transition from classical to quantum encryption methods. Many organizations are not yet prepared for the quantum revolution and continue to rely on encryption techniques that may soon become vulnerable. Governments, corporations, and individuals need to begin adopting quantum-resistant encryption methods to protect their data from future quantum attacks. Early adoption of quantum encryption will be crucial to ensuring the continued security of personal and sensitive information in the years to come.

The Intersection of AI, Quantum Computing, and Privacy

The combination of AI and quantum computing presents unique challenges for data privacy. Both technologies rely on vast amounts of data to function effectively, and depending on how they are implemented, they have the potential to either protect or undermine privacy.

As mentioned earlier, AI systems require large datasets to function, and this data often includes personal information. As AI becomes more sophisticated, it will be able to make more accurate predictions about individuals ' behavior, preferences, and vulnerabilities. This raises significant privacy concerns, mainly when AI systems are used in areas such as law enforcement, healthcare, and financial services.

Quantum computing, on the other hand, has the potential to break current encryption methods, exposing personal data that was previously considered secure. This creates a pressing need for new encryption methods that can withstand quantum attacks.

To protect privacy in this new era, it is essential to adopt a multi-faceted approach that addresses both the technical and ethical challenges posed by AI and quantum computing. This includes developing new privacy-enhancing technologies, updating legal frameworks to reflect the realities of the digital age, and raising public awareness about the risks and benefits of these emerging technologies.

Strategies for Protecting Privacy in the Age of AI and Quantum Computing

As AI and quantum computing continue to advance, it is critical to develop strategies that can effectively protect privacy in this new landscape. Below are several essential approaches that can help safeguard individual privacy:

1. **Quantum-Resistant Encryption**: One of the most urgent priorities in preparing for the quantum era is the development and adoption of quantum-resistant encryption methods. These encryption algorithms are designed to withstand attacks from both classical and quantum computers. Organizations that handle sensitive data, such as financial institutions and healthcare providers, should begin transitioning to quantum-resistant encryption as soon as possible. Governments should also invest in research and development to accelerate the adoption of quantum-secure technologies.

2. **Privacy by Design**: Privacy should be considered from the very beginning when developing AI systems. This means designing systems that collect the minimum amount of personal data necessary for the task at hand and ensuring that this data is anonymized or encrypted whenever possible. Techniques such as differential privacy, which adds noise to datasets to protect individual identities, can also help ensure that personal data remains secure.

3. **Transparency and Accountability in AI**: As AI systems become more prevalent, it is essential to ensure that they are transparent and accountable. This means providing clear explanations of how AI systems make decisions and ensuring that individuals can challenge or appeal these decisions if necessary. Transparency is essential

when AI systems are used in areas such as law enforcement, healthcare, and financial services, where the stakes are high and decisions can significantly impact individuals ' lives.

4. **Updating Legal Frameworks**: Many of the privacy laws in place today were written before the rise of AI and quantum computing; to protect privacy in the digital age, it is essential to update these laws to reflect the new challenges posed by these technologies. For example, new regulations may be needed to govern how AI systems collect and use personal data or to establish standards for the use of quantum encryption in government and corporate settings. Global cooperation will also be essential in creating a consistent legal framework that can protect privacy across borders.

5. **Public Awareness and Education**: Educating the public about the risks and benefits of AI and quantum computing is critical to ensuring informed consent. People need to understand how their data is being collected, how it can be used, and what steps they can take to protect themselves. Governments and corporations should invest in public awareness campaigns to ensure that individuals have the knowledge and tools they need to navigate the digital landscape safely.

6. **Ethical AI Development**: AI systems should be developed in accordance with ethical principles, including respect for privacy and human rights. This means ensuring that AI systems do not discriminate against individuals based on factors such as race, gender, or socioeconomic status and that they are used in ways that promote fairness and equality. Ethical AI development also involves considering the long-term implications of AI systems and ensuring that they are designed to benefit society.

The Future of Privacy in a Quantum and AI-Driven World

As AI and quantum computing continue to develop, the future of privacy will depend on how we implement these technologies. While these technologies have the potential to enhance security and efficiency greatly, they also pose significant risks to personal privacy.

The future of privacy in a quantum and AI-driven world will require a combination of technical innovation, legal reform, and public engagement. By developing privacy-enhancing technologies, adopting new legal frameworks, and raising awareness about the importance of privacy, we can ensure that individuals retain control over their personal information in the digital age.

In the end, the success of these efforts will depend on our ability to strike a balance between the benefits of AI and quantum computing and the need to protect privacy; this will require collaboration between governments, corporations, and individuals and a commitment to ethical principles that prioritize individuals' rights and freedoms.

Final Thoughts: Building a Privacy-Centric Future

The digital revolution brought about by AI and quantum computing offers unprecedented opportunities for innovation, but it also challenges some of our most fundamental rights, including the right to privacy. As we move forward, we must take proactive steps to protect privacy in this new era.

By adopting quantum-resistant encryption, developing privacy-friendly AI systems, and updating legal frameworks, we can build a future where privacy is not sacrificed in the name of progress. At the same time, it is essential to remain vigilant about the potential risks posed by these technologies and to ensure that they are used in ways that benefit society.

The future is bright, but it is also uncertain. The choices we make today about how we develop and implement AI and quantum computing will shape the digital landscape for generations to come. By prioritizing privacy and security, we can ensure that the future of technology respects and protects individuals' rights.

GLOBE WITH CIRCUIT

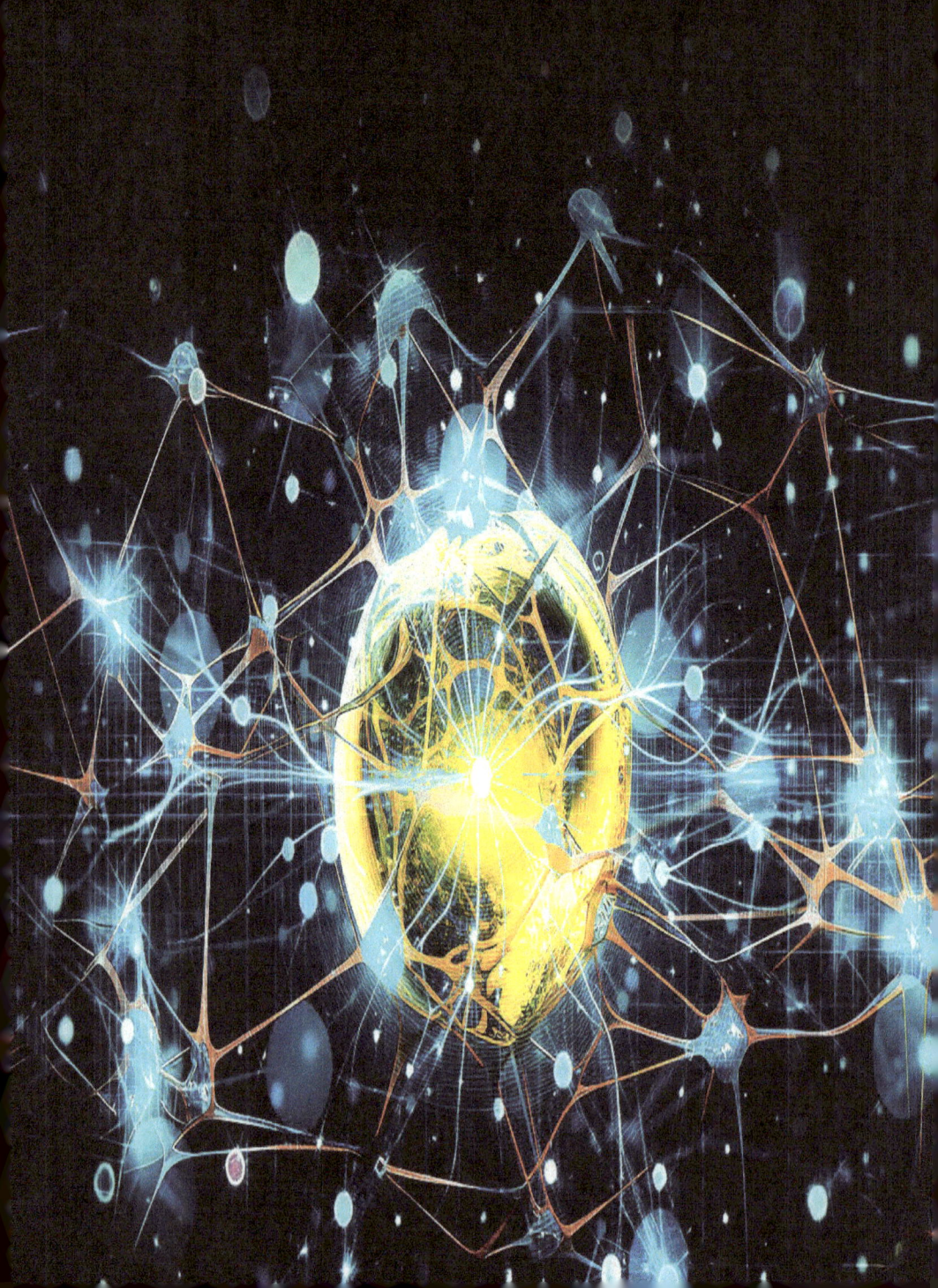

FURTHER READING

1. **"Zero Trust: Proactive Cyber Security for Everyone" by Troy Williams**.

If you're looking to strengthen your understanding of cybersecurity, this book is a great resource. It explains the Zero Trust security model and offers practical, actionable steps for businesses and individuals to protect themselves from cyber threats. It also dives into real-world examples of common scams and how to prevent them, making it highly relevant to today's cybersecurity landscape.

2. **"Unveiling Privacy: Navigating the Data-Driven World" by Troy Williams**.

Privacy in the digital age is more important than ever, and this book lays out the threats to our privacy from corporate surveillance, data breaches, and government overreach. Williams offers easy-to-follow steps for protecting your digital footprint and ensuring your privacy, making it a must-read for anyone concerned about their online security.

3. **"The Future of Artificial Intelligence: A New Dawn" by Troy Williams**.

This forward-looking book discusses AI's growing role in various industries and how AI will shape our future. It covers key trends, including AI's ethical implications, and offers a roadmap for navigating the challenges and opportunities AI presents.

4. **"Cyberpsychology: Understanding Human Behavior in the Digital Age" by Troy Williams.**

This book offers profound insights into the psychological effects of technology on humans. It covers topics such as cyberbullying, internet addiction, and the impact of social media on self-esteem. It's a fascinating read for parents, educators, and anyone who wants to understand the mental effects of our increasingly digital lives.

5. **"Quantum Computing: A Gentle Introduction" by Eleanor G. Rieffel and Wolfgang H. Polak.**

This book offers an approachable introduction to quantum computing, a field that will soon revolutionize data security. It explains the principles of quantum computing in simple terms, making it accessible to readers without a solid technical background. It's ideal for anyone curious about the future of computing and security.

7. **"Privacy in the Age of Big Data: Recognizing Threats, Defending Your Rights, and Protecting Your Family" by Theresa Payton and Ted Claypoole.**

This book is an excellent resource for understanding how big data affects personal privacy. It explores the dangers of corporations and governments collecting data while providing clear strategies for safeguarding your information online. It's perfect for anyone looking to take control of their privacy.

8. **"The Ethics of Artificial Intelligence" by Bostrom and Yudkowsky.**

This comprehensive book examines the moral and ethical challenges posed by the development of AI. It explores potential dangers, including bias and the displacement of jobs, and offers strategies for developing AI technologies that benefit society. It's a valuable resource for understanding the broader implications of AI.

9. "Quantum Computation and Quantum Information" by Michael A. Nielsen and Isaac L. Chuang.

This book is known as the definitive textbook on quantum computing. It is highly detailed and technical. It provides in-depth explanations of quantum algorithms, quantum cryptography, and the future of secure communications, ideal for readers who want a deeper technical understanding of quantum technologies.